Nations and Nationalism in a Global Era

Anthony D. Smith

Polity Press

First published in 1995 by Polity Press in association with Blackwell Publishers Ltd.
Reprinted 1996, 1998, 2000

Editorial office:
Polity Press
65 Bridge Street
Cambridge CB2 1UR, UK

Marketing and production:
Blackwell Publishers Ltd
108 Cowley Road
Oxford OX4 1JF, UK

Published in the USA by
Blackwell Publishers Inc.
350 Main Street
Malden MA 02148, USA

A CIP catalogue record for this book is available from the British Library.

Library of Congress Cataloging-in-Publication Data
Smith, Anthony D.
    Nations and nationalism in a global era / Anthony D. Smith.
        p.   cm.
    Includes bibliographical references (p.   ) and index.
    ISBN 0–7456–1018–8 (cloth : acid-free paper).
    — ISBN 0–7456–1019–6 (pbk. : acid-free paper).
    1. Nationalism.   I. Title.
    JC311.S5393   1995
    320.5'4–dc20   95–10019
                                                                           CIP

Typeset in 11 on 13 pt Sabon by Best-set Typesetter Ltd, Hong Kong
Printed in Great Britain by TJ International, Padstow, Cornwall
This book is printed on acid-free paper.

Contents

v

For we fight not for glory, nor riches, nor honours, but for freedom alone, which no good man gives up except with his life.

Declaration of Arbroath, 1320

Forgetfulness leads to exile, while remembrance is the secret of redemption.

Baal Shem Tov

Preface

Many people throughout the world have been astonished and saddened by the sudden eruption of ethnic conflict and nationalism across the globe. They had hoped for a world free of ethnic dissensions and national conflicts, in the belief that ethnicity and nationalism were being rapidly superseded. They forget that ethnic community has a long history and that nationalism, as an ideology and a movement, has been a powerful force in world politics since at least the French and American Revolutions. The recent resurgence of nationalism can only be understood as part of a long historical process, and analyses that commence with the fall of the Berlin Wall, or even the Second World War, are apt to be shallow and misleading.

My aim in this book is to assess some of the ways in which the resurgence of nationalism today has been analysed, and to offer my own viewpoint on recent trends in the formation of nations and nationalisms, building on ideas briefly adumbrated in the last chapter of my *National Identity* and an earlier article.[1] It is not my purpose to provide a survey of current nationalisms, or to discuss empirical trends in particular parts of the world. The reader will not find here any discussion of current struggles in the former Yugoslavia or the Caucasus or South Africa, nor of the prospects for Sikh, Palestinian or any other nationalism.

Nor do I seek to engage with the wider debates about modernity or 'globalization' and their consequences, except where they touch on issues of national identity and nationalism, since I believe that the key to an understanding of nations and nationalism as general phenomena of the modern world lies more with the persisting frameworks and legacies of historical cultures and ethnic ties than with the consequences of global interdependence. This is not to deny the magnitude of those consequences. Their main effect on modes of human association has been to undermine traditional structures of community and to diffuse the ideology of nationalism, 'disembedding' it from its particular national contexts. But the disembedding of nationalism was already achieved in and through the French Revolution, and it is possible to see nationalism, paradoxically, as one of the main forces for global interdependence.

My argument is rather that nationalism derives its force from its historical embeddedness. As an ideology, nationalism can take root only if it strikes a popular chord, and is taken up by, and inspires, particular social groups and strata. But nationalism is much more than an ideology. Unlike other modern belief-systems, it depends for its power not just on the general idea of the nation, but on the presence and character of this or that specific nation which it turns into an absolute. Its success, therefore, depends on specific cultural and historical contexts, and this means that the nations it helps to create are in turn derived from pre-existing and highly particularized cultural heritages and ethnic formations. This, not some revolutionary but abstract formulation, is what stirs so many men and women in so many corners of the world today. As Benedict Anderson has pointed out, nationalism is far more akin to religion and religious community than to, say, liberalism and socialism. This is the main reason why current 'modernist' and 'post-modernist' critiques of nationalism seem so often to miss their mark, and why it is necessary to look elsewhere for the continuing power and vitality of nations and nationalisms in an interdependent world.

I am very grateful to Anthony Giddens and Polity Press for enabling me to set down my views on what has, once again, become a pressing international, as well as social and cultural, issue. I should like to express my warm thanks to Professors Giovanni Aldobrandini and Maria Damiani Sticchi for inviting me to Rome to give some lectures to students at the Libera Università Internationale degli Studi Soziali which formed the starting-point for these reflections; and to the members of the Association for the Study of Ethnicity and Nationalism, and the Research Workshop on Ethnicity and Nationalism at the London School of Economics, for stimulating conferences, seminars and discussions of recent contributions in the field. For the views contained herein and for any errors, however, the responsibility is mine alone.

Anthony D. Smith,
London School of Economics

Introduction

In this book I want to examine why, at the close of the second millennium, there should be a resurgence of ethnic conflict and nationalism, at a time when the world is becoming more unified and interconnected, and when the barriers between ethnic groups and nations are falling away and becoming obsolete.

We are constantly being reminded that the globe we inhabit is becoming smaller and more integrated. Everywhere closer links are being forged between the economies and societies of our planet, and everywhere formerly independent states and nations are being bound by a complex web of interstate organizations and regulations into a truly international community. In every corner of the world ethnic pasts are being updated and old cultures fragmented and recast. Throughout the world humanity is bound to the wheel of automated technologies and encircled by a forest of mass communications. In short, our world has become a single place.

This 'compression' of time and space has fundamentally changed the ways in which human beings relate to each other and to their social networks. There is no doubt that modernity has brought a revolution in the ways in which we conceive of the world and feel about the societies into which it is divided. Perhaps the moment has at last arrived to realize the hope of Marx and Engels that a common literature and culture can emerge out of the many national cultures and literatures. Perhaps, too, the time has come to remould our political frameworks and ideologies, and sweep away obsolete divisions and ancient antagonisms, in line with the emerging international division of labour in which trade barriers are falling away and commodities and labour are able to move freely across continents. The same revolution has brought about the collapse of ancient traditions and religious values and has compelled many people to separate practices and beliefs from their former contexts and to incorporate a diversity of others – other cultures, other peoples, other ways of life – into self-images and social relations.[1]

But this is only one side of the contemporary picture. The other is represented by the rise and proliferation of all kinds of social movement and identity protest, from feminism to the ecology movement, from the civil rights movement to religious revivals. In particular, we are witnessing a rebirth of ethnic nationalism, of religious fundamentalisms and of group antagonisms which were thought to have been long buried. Ethnic protests for autonomy and secession, wars of national irredentism and explosive racial conflicts over labour markets and social facilities have proliferated in every continent. In the era of globalization and transcendence, we find ourselves caught in a maelstrom of conflicts over political identities and ethnic fragmentation. In India, the Caucasus, the Balkans, the Horn of Africa and southern Africa, bloody conflicts have erupted, and even in more stable and affluent societies like Canada, Great Britain, Belgium, Spain, France, Italy and Germany, the tremors of popular ethnic movements and xenophobic racism and nationalism are felt periodically. For many people a 'narrow', fissiparous nationalism has become the greatest source of political danger in the contemporary world, while everywhere ethnic and national identities remain highly charged and sensitive political issues.

How can this paradox be explained? Is it an inevitable product of a dialectic of cultural globalization which produces a new kind of identity politics in the wake of the disembedding revolution of modernity, or just a 'survival' from an earlier age of nationalist hatreds and wars? Is it simply a temporary aberration, which further capitalist or post-industrial progress will iron out in area after area? Or is this contradiction of modern culture likely to grow and intensify as it spreads across the globe?

There have been three main solutions to this paradox. The first suggests that contemporary nations and nationalisms are the epigoni of their illustrious predecessors, survivals from another epoch, which are destined to pass away once they have run their course in each part of the globe. This may take a few decades and cause much suffering and bloodshed, but essentially such ethnic nationalisms and racisms, however much they appear to proliferate and engulf successive regions of the world in the short term, are of no lasting consequence. They will soon be depoliticized and 'normalized'. In any case, they are not part of the great movements of history, the chariot of progress which is tied to the great structures and motors of historical change – the international division of labour, great regional markets, powerful military blocs, electronic communications, computerized information technology, mass public education, the mass media, the sexual revolution and the like. These are the forces of the future, and the accompanying trend to the small-scale and intimate is no more than a comforting diversion or smokescreen for the growing inclusiveness and resource maximization of human communities. In fact, we are already witnessing the breakdown of the 'homogenous nation' in many societies, whose cultures and narratives of national identity are becoming increasingly hybridized and ambivalent, and the emergence, some would say re-emergence, of looser polyethnic societies.

A 'post-modern' era, like its 'pre-modern' counterpart, has little place for politicized ethnicity or for nationalism as an autonomous political force.[2]

A second argument is that nations and nationalisms are inevitable products, and producers, of modernity. Modernization, usually dated from the French and Industrial Revolutions (and sometimes from the Reformation), has transformed our whole way of life to a degree and in a manner unknown since the Neolithic Revolution and the birth of settled agriculture. Industrial capitalism, the bureaucratic state, total warfare, mass social mobilization, science and rationalism, mass computerized information and electronic communications, the breakdown of traditional family values and the sexual revolution, have altered the lives of every individual on the planet and thrown them out of their habitual practices and daily routines. New ways and unorthodox life-styles have disorientated and dislocated groups and individuals alike, destroying old structures and rendering ancient cultures obsolete. The revolution of modernization has brought very considerable fragmentation, but also new modes of communication and integration based on the new electronic technologies of information and dissemination. In this unprecedented situation, nations and nationalisms are necessary, if unpalatable, instruments for controlling the destructive effects of massive social change; they provide the only large-scale and powerful communities and belief-systems that can secure a mimimum of social cohesion, order and meaning in a disruptive and alienating world. Moreover, they are the only popular forces that can legitimate and make sense of the activities of that most powerful modern agent of social transformation, the rational state. For this reason nations and nationalisms are unlikely to disappear, at least until all areas of the globe have made the painful transition to an affluent and stable modernity, on the Western model.[3]

A third view claims that nations and nationalisms are perennial. They are neither survivals of a nationalist era about to be swept away or disintegrate, nor inevitable if regrettable products of modernity. On the contrary, it is modernity and the so-called 'post-modern' era that will pass away, while nations remain as the bedrock of human society. Nations and nationalism are the basic forces and processes of the modern as well as the pre-modern epochs, while modernization and modernity are really only the modes by which nations are realized in the contemporary world. For some, including many nationalists, this is part and parcel of a 'primordial' natural order; the members of a given nation may have been induced to 'forget' their nation and its (usually glorious) history, but nature will in the end reassert itself and the nation will be 'reborn'. For others, nations perform general human functions, providing social cohesion, order, warmth and the like; that is why particular nations, though no part of any 'natural order', seem to their members to be all-embracing and immemorial, and we in turn must admit the power and enduring quality of the fundamental cultural ties. Either way, the ethnic community and the nation remain essential building-blocks of any conceivable new order. Though their forms may undergo change, the substance of ethnic and national ties will persist beneath whatever social and political transformations may supervene.[4]

None of these viewpoints, in my opinion, does justice to the complexity of the situation. They are flawed on general grounds, and as guides to the paradox of global interdependence and fissiparous nationalism. Rather than viewing nations and nationalisms as obsolete survivals of an earlier, more insular era, or as inevitable products of global modernization and late capitalism, or as perennial and natural features of human history and society, we must trace them back to their underlying ethnic and territorial contexts; we must set them in the wider historical intersection between cultural ties and political communities, as these were influenced by, and influenced, the processes of administrative centralization, economic transformation, mass communications and the dis-integration of traditions which we associate with modernity. Both the longer time-frame and the recovery of the ethnic substratum are needed if we are to make sense of the ubiqui-tous appeal and enduring hold of national ideals at a time in history when other forces seem to presage, and hasten, the obsolescence of nationalism.

Accordingly, I will start by considering the approaches of those who see nations being transcended by globalization and a global culture, and the limitations of their analyses of ethnicity and nationalism. This is followed by an examin-ation of the merits and fallacies of the modernist arguments, with some empirical counter-examples. Finally, the peren-nialist position is revealed as both untenable and significant. Each of these viewpoints, I shall argue, highlights some im-portant dimensions of current developments, but each is limited. The 'global culture' approach goes well beyond the evidence and fails to grasp the import of proliferating ethnic nationalisms. The modernist approach is more realistic and firmly grounded, but it too lacks historical depth and specificity. The perennialist claim, on the other hand, has little explanatory power, though it draws attention to the need for a wider historical framework.

That framework forms the basis for an alternative ap-proach which I believe to be both fuller and more convincing than its rivals. From this point of view, the problem is seen as stemming from the mutual influence of 'layers' of social and historical experience, and the derivation of national phenom-ena from ethnic and territorial symbolism and modes of organization. It therefore draws on a wide range of historical evidence of human association and identity to illuminate the underlying problem of the emotional depth and social hold of nationalism which continues to puzzle all who involve them-selves in this field. This will also enable us to confront the paradox of fragmentation in a globalizing era from a deeper socio-historical standpoint.

INTRODUCTION

Only by grasping the power of nationalism and the continuing appeal of national identity through their rootedness in pre-modern ethnic symbolism and modes of organization is there some chance of understanding the resurgence of ethnic nationalism at a time when 'objective' conditions might appear to render it obsolete. Without such understanding, we shall remain bewildered onlookers of unpredictable political dramas in a world of contradictory trends and antagonistic forces.

1

A Cosmopolitan Culture?

In his study of the evolution of nationalism, mainly in Europe, Eric Hobsbawm claims that the phenomenon of late twentieth-century nationalist, or ethnic politics, is 'functionally different from the "nationalism" and the "nations" of nineteenth- and earlier twentieth-century history. It is no longer a major vector of historical development.'[1]

The building of nations around national states and industrial economies in the nineteenth century, and the anti-colonial movements of national liberation and emancipation of the mid-twentieth century were both, he claims, central to historical development. But this is not the case with the ethnic and linguistic nationalisms that emerged in the second half of the nineteenth century, and which continue to proliferate today. Nation-building and national liberation movements were 'typically unificatory as well as emancipatory', whereas the characteristic late twentieth-century nationalisms are 'essentially negative, or rather divisive. Hence the insistence on "ethnicity" and linguistic differences, each or both sometimes combined with religion.'

In line with classical Marxist analysis, Hobsbawm regards these movements as having links with earlier 'small-nationality movements directed against the Habsburg, Tsarist and Ottoman empires'. But, in another sense, they are quite the opposite, a rejection of modern modes of political organization, based on

> reactions of weakness and fear, attempts to erect barricades to keep at bay the forces of the modern world, similar in this respect to the resentment of Prague Germans pressed into a corner by Czech immigration rather than to that of the advancing Czechs.[2]

These fears have been fuelled by recent international population movements and rapid, fundamental socio-economic transformations. Hobsbawm cites the examples of Estonian, Welsh and Quebecois responses to Russian and Anglophone immigration, and adds: 'Wherever we live in an urbanised society, we encounter strangers: uprooted men and women who remind us of the fragility, or the drying up of our own families' roots.'[3] He goes on to explain, in terms drawn from Simmel's analysis of group conflict, that

> The call of ethnicity or language provides no guidance to the future at all. It is merely a protest against the status quo or, more precisely, against 'the others' who threaten the ethnically defined group.

For:

> nationalism by definition excludes from its purview all who do not belong to its own 'nation', i.e. the vast majority of the human race. Moreover, while fundamentalism can, at least to some extent, appeal to what remains of genuine custom and tradition or past practice as embodied in religious practice, as we have seen nationalism in itself is either hostile to the real ways of the past, or arises on its ruins.[4]

Why, then, have ethnic and linguistic nationalisms become so prevalent today? Because, according to Hobsbawm, they constitute 'a response to the overwhelmingly non-national and non-nationalist principles of state formation in the greater part of the twentieth-century world'. But this does not mean that ethnic reactions can provide any alternative principle for the political restructuring of the world in the twenty-first century.[5]

Echoing a now familiar theme, Hobsbawm argues that the principles of such a restructuring have little to do with nations or nationalism. This is because nations have lost their former economic functions, though he concedes that large *states* will continue to exercise important economic functions. But in general global interdependence means that much larger economic units will provide the bases of community in the future. For Hobsbawm, it is axiomatic that nationalism 'is nothing without the creation of nation-states, and a world of such states, fitting the present ethnic-linguistic criteria of nationality, is not a feasible prospect today'.[6]

Given this principle, it follows that as an ethnic or linguistic phenomenon,

> in spite of its evident prominence, nationalism today is historically less important. It is no longer, as it were, a global political programme, as it may have been in the nineteenth and early twentieth centuries. It is at most a complicating factor, or a catalyst for other developments.

Retreating before, or adapting to, the new 'supranational restructuring of the globe', 'Nations and nationalism will be present in this history but in subordinate, and often rather minor roles.' Taking his cue from Elie Kedourie, Hobsbawm is able to conclude that, with historians now making rapid progress in analysing the phenomena of nations and nationalism, this suggests that

> as so often, the phenomenon is past its peak. The owl of Minerva which brings wisdom, said Hegel, flies out at dusk. It is a good sign that it is now circling round nations and nationalism.[7]

Depoliticizing the nation

Hobsbawm's analysis is one of many predicting the early demise of nations and nationalism. It represents a Marxist variant of this reading, with its differentiation of a positive, unifying (but nineteenth-century) nationalism and a negative, divisive (but contemporary) nationalism. This follows the historical distinction which Hobsbawm, consonant with that of Marx and Engels, draws between two kinds of European and non-European nationalism. The first, which flourished from 1830 to 1870, is a democratic mass political nationalism of the 'great nations' stemming from the citizenship ideals of the French Revolution. The second, characteristic of the period from 1870 to 1914, by contrast, is a narrow ethnic or linguistic nationalism, a small-nationality reaction to the obsolete polities of the Ottoman, Habsburg and Tsarist empires among mainly peripheral peoples in often backward areas.[8]

In the second half of the nineteenth century, according to Hobsbawm, urbanization, mass migrations and the new theories of 'race' gave the activities of romantic intellectuals a new political significance and mass support among the 'lesser examination-passing classes'. This led to the vogue for ethnic or linguistic (or ethno-linguistic) nationalism, the kind of nationalism, so irrelevant to a global era of large-scale economies and polities, that continues to fire people's imaginations, or rather to answer to their fears and weaknesses. The older, democratic political nationalism, having done its historical work and run its course, has been superseded by the spate of more recent ethno-linguistic nationalisms, which are little more than reactionary or bewildered responses to the rapidity of global changes. But they too will soon wilt and fade in the face of the inexorable large-scale politico-economic movements of world history.

Now this kind of optimistic materialist evolutionism is not confined to Marxists. It informs liberal critiques of nationalism, from Carr and Kohn to Smelser and Breuilly. Basically, all these critiques accept the persisting reality and historic role of the large-scale national state, but seek to depoliticize it, to render it harmless, by turning the nation into a purely cultural or folkloristic phenomenon stripped of all political significance, in the interests of wider segments of humanity or of humanity as a whole.[9]

One way to achieve this depoliticization is to separate the cultural level of the nation from the political level of the state, or better, from the regional economic association of states. Only the latter possess 'real' social and political importance in the evolving world order, since the 'nation-state' can no longer contain within its boundaries both a territorial market and a mass, public culture. Having lost both these public functions, the nation sinks to the level of 'ethnicity' and 'culture' or 'folklore' – a purely romantic attachment to the past, matching the romanticized cultural expressiveness of some scholarly approaches. It loses all its erstwhile political dimensions.[10]

A second way to depoliticize the nation is to demilitarize it. The nation, whether wedded to a particular state or not, is no longer the effective actor in the international arena, because in the contemporary world it is existentially bound to its neighbours or to a regional military bloc and can have no really independent defence or foreign policy. The nation-state is no longer free to conduct its external relations as it desires; it is bound not only by general, international norms such as those of the UN Charter, but also by specific regional treaties and associations into which it finds itself willy-nilly drawn. With the loss of its military guarantee, national sovereignty is radically curtailed, if not abolished.

Third, the nation can be 'normalized' and its nationalism ritualized. Through the United Nations, by means of international fora and conferences, multilateral agreements and organizations and the like, the national aspirations of each nation are legitimated and thereby tamed. They become part of the global framework of assumptions and the international institutional order. The fangs of nationalism are thereby drawn, and a benign and healthy national identity or patriotism with its replicated symbolism of flags, anthems and ceremonial parades is *de rigueur*. Within the comity of equal nations, nationalism has been stripped of its political force and reduced to the symbolic level, and to peaceful economic, artistic and sports competitions.

What all these ways have in common is the idea of sundering the nation from the political domain and returning it to the sphere of culture and civil society from which it sprang, as if thereby the evil genie could be sealed once again in his proverbial bottle. Unfortunately, such an idea betrays a serious misunderstanding of the nature of nationalism. It assumes that cultural nationalism and political nationalism are not only separate phenomena, they are unrelated to each other. But this is to miss an essential element of the power of nationalism, its chameleon-like ability to transmute itself according to the perceptions and needs of different communities and of competing strata, factions and individuals within them. It is also crucially to misunderstand the relationship between culture and politics in nationalism. Nationalism cannot be reduced to the uniform principle that the cultural unit must be made congruent with the political unit. Not only does this omit a number of other vital nationalist tenets, it fails to grasp the fact that the development of any nationalism depends on bringing the cultural and moral regeneration of the community into a close relationship, if not harmony, with the political mobilization and self-determination of its members. Hence, the idea that nationalism can be 'returned' to any sphere, even that of culture, is both naive and fundamentally misconceived. This is to remove the mainspring of nationalism, the ideal of communal regeneration in any and every sphere of human life, and substitute the 'pure form' of the territorial nation for its emotional content – on the lines of that

13

other hollow strategy, 'national in form, socialist in content . . .'.[11]

Empirically, too, the fact that nationalism continually reappears in different parts of the world, even among federal states and more advanced societies, suggests how dangerously misconceived and misleading is the belief that depoliticizing the nation can provide the cure for aggressive nationalisms. Indeed, Hobsbawm's concluding admission that ethno-linguistic nationalisms have once again reappeared and are flourishing everywhere, even in highly industrialized states, undermines his earlier argument that nations and nationalism are being superseded by the transnational forces of late modernity. That it is the wealthier, more educationally endowed parts of states that often opt for radical autonomy or even secession – the Punjab in India, the Baltic states in the former Soviet Union, Slovenia and Croatia in the former Yugoslavia, Catalonia, the Basque country and Quebec – and continue to do so after nationalism has been on the political scene for some two hundred years – must give even the most hardened or optimistic of evolutionists pause. With the fate of so many polyethnic and multinational states hanging in the balance, it would be a bold person who could make out a case today for the success of 'plural nations' on the American or Australian model. It would be nearer the mark to suggest that ethnic nationalisms are making the running in contemporary state-making, and that the political nationalisms of national states and the ethnic nationalisms of its ethnic communities coexist uneasily or are locked in conflict with each other, a situation that has obtained at least since 1945 and shows no signs of abating or being resolved.[12]

Nor is there much sign of the demilitarization of nations. True, the nuclear superpowers are making deep cuts in their huge arsenals of weapons, but new dangers of nuclear proliferation in Kazakhstan, the Ukraine, Israel, India, Pakistan and North Korea have been accompanied by massive increases in weapons sales, especially to combatants in troubled areas, and continuing heavy expenditure by many states on military budgets. Many states, even in the European Community, remain firmly wedded to an independent defence and foreign policy, fed today by new concerns over terrorism, epidemics, narcotics and mass immigration. Fears of immigrant waves have fuelled resentments, and spurred renewed interest in cultural identity, national solidarity and defence of national interests, concerns that are turned by extremists into xenophobic racism and anti-Semitism and by more moderate groups into a reaffirmation of a defensive state nationalism. The many violent breaches of a once-vaunted 'new world order' within the last few years – in Iraq, Bosnia, Somalia, South Africa, the Caucasus and elsewhere – have forced national states to reassess their military and security commitments and attitudes, with the result that in most cases each national state has acted in what its elites perceived to be its national interests.

Nor has the promotion of normalization damped down the 'fires of nationalism'. While nationalism has been accorded a general global legitimacy, at least in the right of self-determination written into the UN Charter (though applied only to ex-colonies), it is simultaneously excoriated, or at least the manifestations of other peoples' nationalisms continue to be routinely denounced. Though there is widespread acceptance of the nation as the only basis for political action and mass mobilization, nationalism, the ideology and movement, remains suspect, and national separatism is generally frowned on. Nor has the idea of harnessing 'unbridled nationalism' by binding together the nations of particular regions in economic and political associations met with much success. This is not to say that many national states do not cooperate on a variety of political and practical projects all over the world, as they have done in the past. But that is no guarantee against sudden irruptions of national fervour or ethnic separatism, whenever international circumstances permit and social conditions encourage it.[13]

All of which points to the emptiness of the predictions, and the failures of policies for, transcending the nation and superseding nationalism through measures of 'depoliticization'. These measures have a fairly long history, stretching back to the League of Nations. Their repeated failure may not be sufficient to undermine widespread evolutionary approaches to nationalism (which nationalism itself has encouraged), but they should put us on our guard against the more sweeping claims of their proponents about the inevitable 'movement of history' and the irreversible forces of globalization.

New imperialisms?

Underlying both the socialist and the liberal evolutionist viewpoints has been the assumption that the large-scale nation or 'great nation' (always a national state) was the sole vehicle of social and political progress and that, once it had performed its world-historical role of bringing all peoples into the civilizing process, it would be superseded by even larger and more powerful units of human association. A staging-post in the ascent of humanity, the great nation would gracefully or otherwise cede place to the continental and regional association or community. This brings us to the idea of a 'new imperialism'.[14]

In the more recent versions of the argument, the primary agents of world-historical progress are the huge transnational companies, the great power blocs and the vast systems of mass communications that encircle the globe. For theorists of 'advanced capitalism' in its global phase, it is the great transnational companies with their huge budgets, armies of skilled personnel, massive investments, far-flung markets and advanced technologies, that are the main carriers of capitalist modernity. Their dominant position and preponderance over all but the largest states represents a new stage of capitalism, but their operations also require both a transnational class of capitalists and a powerful global ideology and culture of mass consumerism, with all its familiar ideas and practices of mass advertising, packaging and material inducements which draw more and more populations and countries into the transnational domain. These practices, ideas and images, disembedded from any context, are like currencies, interchangeable in the world market of consumer culture, with the result that the national state and national identities are bypassed and relativized.[15]

Theories of 'post-industrialism' have been more impressed by the political potential of new systems of electronic mass communications. These vast networks of telecommunications, with their great advances in sophisticated computerized information technology, coupled with the impact of the new generation of visual mass media, have of course promoted the standardized packaging of products, images and markets of the transnational companies. But they have also enabled powerful international organizations like the IMF or World Bank to emerge and compete with all but the largest national states, and have suggested possibilities for a new cosmopolitan global culture, leaping over national boundaries and free of national limitations. It seems that where Esperanto failed, information technology might succeed.[16]

But there is another possibility. The new systems of mass communications – radio, television, videos, personal computers – are also encouraging much smaller social and political groups and ethnic and linguistic communities to create and sustain their own dense social and cultural networks, in opposition both to national states and to a wider continental or global culture. This is one, perhaps unexpected, source of that resurgence of ethnic nationalisms, not least in its advanced core, which Hobsbawm and others decry, but which continue to multiply under the umbrella of wider, looser associations like the European Union and their overarching ideologies.[17]

Now the dream of global unity is not new. It goes back to those universal empires – of Hammurabi and Alexander, Justinian and Harun al-Rashid, Genghis Khan and Charles V, Napoleon and the British Empire – which saw and proclaimed themselves to be the carriers of civilization and regarded others as backward savages and barbarians. They too presented themselves as universal sacred civilizations, holding sway over the known world and carried through an elite language and a 'high' culture that knew no boundaries – despite the fact that the great mass of their populations lived their lives in much smaller cultural orbits, only intermittently touched by these great traditions.

Today, of course, this old-fashioned imperialism has been invalidated, driven back by an assertive nationalism, though not abolished. The devotees of a global culture are far from desiring any association with such aspirations, even in their mildest cultural variants. Their cultural relativism and their forthright ecumenical cosmopolitanism stand in sharp opposition not only to a divisive nationalism, but also to aggressive and self-aggrandizing imperialisms of all kinds.

But can a global culture avoid cultural imperialism? Can it become truly cosmopolitan? Is not English, for example, increasingly the global *lingua franca*? Have not European (mainly French and British) institutions and American life-styles come to define much of what passes for an international culture, the culture of Dallas, pop and jeans, but also of computer technology, the mass media, modernist urban architecture, constitutional law and democracy and social justice? Even those near-universal ideological frameworks, capitalism and socialism, were tied to a specific historical context, particular state formations and distinct regional power blocs, based respectively on American and Russian hegemony. Can we escape the specificity of a new imperialism, of a new Pax Americana or Japonica or Europeana, beneath the cosmopolitan cloak of a global culture? Too often, the examples of the global culture which are chosen to illustrate its growth turn out to owe their origins and much of their appeal to the power and prestige of one or other of the great metropolitan power centres and cultures of the contemporary world, the new 'cultural empires' of modernity. This suggests, at least, that the quest for a global culture and the ideal of cosmopolitanism are continually subverted by the realities of power politics and by the nature and features of culture.[18]

A memory-less culture?

But let us for the moment try to picture a genuinely non-imperial global culture, one that is not tied to a particular time or place, and that does not mask a national origin and character. Such a cosmopolitanism is sometimes regarded as a natural concomitant or product of a 'post-modern' culture. Without going into the vexed question of the varieties and meanings to be attributed to 'post-modernism' in various spheres, what appears to be meant by the juxtaposition of globalism and post-modernism is a movement of cultural eclecticism and ambivalence or a pastiche of localized particulars married to a standardized and streamlined scientific technology. On the one hand, there is the playful, sometimes satirical use of various traditional styles, images and words quarried from older historical cultures in literature, music, the arts, architecture and fashion, seen from the standpoint of the medium; on the other hand, there is the unifying veneer of a streamlined, uniform 'scientific' discourse responding to the properties of a technical communications infrastructure.[19]

Indeed, for some, the narration of the nation itself, and especially the concept of the people today, partakes of this hybrid, eclectic character. It is formed from the 'shreds and patches' of historical cultures, and characterized by a 'double time' and a split between the authoritative historical, and pedagogical, narrative of the people and the repetitive, performative narrative of signification which occurs in everyday life and through which the people are reproduced. In this scenario, 'national identity' has become hybridized and ambivalent: it is an assemblage of tales told by all kinds of social groups and individuals, especially the marginalized and the outsider, the immigrant, the ex-colonized, the exiled and the subaltern. Presumably a global culture would be equally hybrid in character, with a number of ambivalent, even contradictory, components: a pastiche of traditional local, folk and national motifs and styles; a modern scientific, quantitative and technical discourse; a culture of mass consumerism consisting of standardized mass commodities, images, practices and slogans; and an interdependence of all these elements across the globe, based upon the unifying pressures of global telecommunications and computerized information systems.[20]

In practice, of course, a hybrid cosmopolitan culture would possess both 'modern' and 'post-modern' features. We would expect it to display both the rationalist, technical and scientific discourse of modernity, but also the ambivalent and nostalgic, if cynical and artificial, manipulation of a plural hybridized past, with its folk traditions and its national languages and cultures, which distinguishes the 'post-modern' reaction to modernity. And all of this would rest on the uniform quantitative and technological base of increasingly sophisticated computerized information networks and electronic mass-communications systems.

In this conception, a hybrid global culture has three features which mark it off as truly novel: it is universal, it is technical and it is timeless. It is universal in the sense that not even the most far-flung empire and its 'cosmopolitan' culture could ever be. Neither the Chinese, nor the Roman, nor the Buddhist, nor the Islamic civilizations could ever pretend to that universality; there were always other empires, and contrasting cultures, at their *limes*. They were always emanations of the properties of specific peoples at definite periods of their history; however attenuated they became, they were always tied to particular places and times, and usually carried by conquering armies. Even great civilizations like Islam and Christianity, which John Armstrong views as matrices of cultural symbols for a number of smaller ethnic communities, betrayed the character of their birthplace or seat of authority. Today's or tomorrow's global culture, on the other hand, even if it is more advanced in America and Western Europe, cannot easily be rooted in time and place. It has lost much of its spatial and temporal specificity in the patchwork of elements of which it is composed, and will surely lose more. It will become truly planetary.[21]

Today's global culture is also the first purely technical civilization. Its use of ethnic or national elements is affectively neutral. Its pastiche is playful and calculated, draining the passion out of issues and reducing them to technical puzzles with purely technical solutions. Its cosmopolitanism reflects its uniform technological base, with its many systems of communications that create interdependent social networks, expressing themselves in an identical standardized, technical, and often quantitative, discourse. This is why a technical intelligentsia has become crucial to late modernity, and why it supplants the earlier humanistic and often nationalist intellectuals. It is the technicians who must man and operate the global mass-communications systems and it is their technical culture of critical discourse which determines the specific character of an emergent global culture.[22]

Besides, a global culture is without time. Forever pursuing an elusive present, an artificial and standardized universal culture has no historical background, no developmental rhythm, no sense of time and sequence. Contextless and timeless, this artificial global culture may quarry the past for illustrative purposes or cynically use motifs from particular pasts with eclectic caprice, but it refuses to locate itself in history. Stripped of any sense of development beyond the performative present, and alien to all ideas of 'roots', the genuine global culture is fluid, ubiquitous, formless and historically shallow.

Why do people imagine and fear the coming of such a rootless, cosmopolitan culture? Could it ever really sustain itself? They imagine and fear its coming because of the rapid advance of those large blocs, those huge transnational companies and mass-communications systems, and the accompanying culture of mass consumerism mentioned above. There is, after all, plenty of evidence of growing cultural and economic uniformity in all sorts of spheres and products. The advance of American mass culture, of the English language, of pop culture, of the visual mass media and computerized information technology, clearly represent significant global cultural trends. These trends are, in all likelihood, here to stay, at least for some decades. But what do they add up to? Can large numbers of men and women live *by* them, as well as *with* them? Do they amount to a new culture, a new lifestyle that is also a way of life, one that can inspire as well as comfort human beings for loss and grief and death? What memories, which myths and symbols, values and identities, can such a global culture offer?

For these are, after all, what past cultures have always sought to provide. Unlike a historically shallow, memory-less global culture, based presumably on the performative discourse of everyday life practices, the cultures of the past were also built around the shared memories, traditions, myths and symbols of successive generations of cultural or political units of population, of a class, a region, a polity, an ethnic or religious community, which they sought to crystallize and express. Unlike a demythologized and ambivalent cosmopolitan culture of the here and now, the cultures of the past were formed on the basis of archetypal myths and symbols, values and memories, told, retold and re-enacted by successive generations of each such culture-community. Unlike a value-neutral and traditionless future culture of the globe, the many particular cultures of the past and present sought always to preserve what Max Weber called their 'irreplaceable culture values', and the particular symbols, rituals, ideals and traditions of those who forged and participated in them.[23]

But perhaps the cosmopolitan culture of the future should not be measured by the standards of earlier time-bound cultures, with all their limitations and particularisms. By definition, rooted past cultures ruled themselves out from the universality necessary for a global culture of the whole of humanity, whatever their pretensions may have been. This is undoubtedly correct as far as it goes. But is there any evidence that we can forge a truly universal culture that can have the appeal, and meet the needs, of human beings all over the world in ways that are equivalent to those of past cultures? Does not the use by a would-be global culture of motifs and images from the many particular ethnic and national pasts suggest that these cultures continue to inform our sensibilities and permeate our social structures? Could we imagine ourselves escaping sufficiently from our pervasive, living pasts with all their beliefs and assumptions, and starting afresh, as it were, on the great enterprise of constructing the timeless, technical, universal global culture? And does this not also suggest that a global culture would not, after all, constitute the radical break with the nationalist past that its proponents seem so to believe and desire it to be, and that the best that can be hoped for in the twenty-first century is that we shall attain to that national 'diversity in unity' that some Euro-federalists have preached?

The fact remains that cultures are historically specific, and so is their imagery. The packaged imagery of the visionary global culture is either trivial and shallow, a matter of mass-commodity advertisement, or it is rooted in existing historical cultures, drawing from them whatever meanings and power it may derive. These cultures of past and present express the experiences of particular social groups that appear just below the surface of the well-packaged imagery of the derivative, hybridized mass-commodity civilization. For a time we may be able to get by and 'invent traditions' and manufacture myths. But if myths and traditions are to be sustained, they must resonate among large numbers of people over several generations, and this means they must belong to the collective experience and memory of particular social groups. So new traditions, too, must be culture-specific: they must be able to appeal to and mobilize members of particular groups while excluding, by implication, outsiders, if they are to maintain themselves beyond the generation of their founders.[24]

In short, a timeless global culture answers to no living needs and conjures no memories. If memory is central to identity, we can discern no global identity in-the-making, nor aspirations for one, nor any collective amnesia to replace existing 'deep' cultures with a cosmopolitan 'flat' culture. The latter remains a dream confined to some intellectuals. It strikes no chord among the vast mass of peoples divided into their habitual communities of class, gender, region, religion and culture.

Images, identities, cultures, all express the plurality and particularism of histories and their remoteness from any new imperialism and any vision of a cosmopolitan global order. The failure of hegemonic powers to control the nationalisms of embattled ethnic communities or of aroused national states runs parallel to the constant reassertion of communal or national autonomy against the demands and inducements of cultural imperialism and of a timeless mass-commodity cosmopolitanism. Whether it be in the sphere of the mass media, or the arts, education or daily life-styles, the claims of elite cultural imperialism and cosmopolitanism are constantly being contested and their boundaries redrawn, beneath the near-universal acceptance of mass-consumer products. In each case, those claims and demands are contextualized by the traditions and perceptions of the recipient community, as successive generations of indigenous intelligentsia seek to accommodate for themselves and their communities the respective demands of Westernization and autochthonous culture. In this chronic cultural warfare, the concept of the nation plays a key role.[25]

Conclusion

Two assumptions underlie all these arguments. The first is one of scale. For Marx and Hobsbawm, nationalism historically presupposed a nation that had an economic 'threshold', i.e. it could play host to a modern capitalist economy, because it possessed a population and territorial scale sufficient for economic viability as well as political independence. It ensured a large territorial market for trade and investments, for labour and commodity production. Even if the territory in question did not possess its own natural resources, at least not in sufficient quantity, it could sustain a population that had the necessary skills to manufacture mass commodities for less developed areas of the world. Such an economic criterion ruled out mini-nations as viable political units; indeed, it rendered them irksome thorns on the road of capitalist progress.[26]

Just this social and political progress was the historic achievement of classical Western mass political nationalisms from the time of the French Revolution until the 1860s. The assumption was that nations that could meet this economic and political criterion, that could furnish territorial markets for advanced capitalism and its mass culture, had and still have a central role to play in the development of political power and geo-political relations. They contributed decisively and disproportionately (if exploitatively) to the international division of labour. Nations that failed to meet the criterion of economic and political viability could play no part in the great movement of history, and their incorporation into the globalizing capitalist economy through the brief moment of their political independence marked their imminent demise as separate and self-determining political nations, a view to which a good many nationalists (usually from one or other 'great nation') have subscribed. In this sense, nationalism was indeed the 'nervous tic' of capitalism.[27]

The trouble with this view, of course, is that, whatever may have been the case in the nineteenth century when capitalism required heavy industry and a vast unskilled proletariat, today's kind of advanced capitalism (or 'post-industrialism') requires instead large service industries, highly skilled labour and sophisticated information technology, thereby encouraging the reverse trends towards flexible specialization, diversification and interdependent networks. As a result, the absence of 'economic viability' and a limited size and scale in the would-be nation have not stood in the way of smaller cultural communities seeking autonomy or maintaining political and economic independence, once it has been achieved. Iceland, Portugal, Norway, Switzerland, Singapore, Taiwan, New Zealand, Israel and Tunisia are just some of the smaller national states whose independence has not been significantly hampered by limitations of size and scale (though lack of natural resources has proved a handicap in some cases); neither has their relative prosperity, although certainly dependent on the wider system of advanced capitalism (as whose prosperity is not?), required or encouraged the diminution of their political independence or cultural distinctiveness. On the contrary, in the eyes of small-nation nationalists, political independence has proved a singular economic boon. It has allowed them the chance to choose between rival great-power offers of aid-and-trade, alliance-and-defence, playing one power off against another, in a manner that colonial status or incorporation as a province in a wider empire or federation would have made quite impossible.[28]

Moreover, it is often the smaller, but economically wealthier and more productive communities and areas, especially in the affluent West or in the European states, that have recently sought or are seeking political independence, a situation that has recently been more widely, if still reluctantly and cautiously, accepted by the international community. This is true of such communities as Quebec, Euzkadi, Catalonia, the Czech Republic, Slovenia, Croatia and the Baltic states, as well as Singapore, Taiwan and Kuwait. Size and scale, therefore, have become much less important in the moral economy of nations in the contemporary world, whereas political independence has remained an important intrinsic value and goal of ethnic communities in every continent.[29]

If Hobsbawm's viewpoint is in this respect essentially conditioned by the classical experiences of nationalism in the nineteenth century and the early part of the twentieth, it is also caught up in that other mistaken nineteenth-century assumption, economic reductionism. What the twentieth century has surely taught us is that we should resist arguments that suggest that different levels of culture – or cultures – will, or must, conform to or be functional for certain kinds and stages of economic and political structures, and that global economic and political trends must be matched (after an appropriate time-lag) by corresponding changes in the scale, organization and type of cultural unit. The scale, budgets, technology, personnel and scope of the operations of economic organizations have been vastly augmented in the last few decades, but it does not follow that the nature, scale and operations of political units, much less of cultural ones, must undergo commensurate changes. They belong to different domains and each has its own processes and trends specific to that domain. In the cultural domain, mass communications have opened up new possibilities for small-scale networks and cultural communities to increase their social density and raise the level of their grassroots participation, at the same time as the number of power centres, and the scale of economic organizations, has grown. There is in fact little match between increasing technological scale and economic success on the one hand and the rise of ethnic nationalisms in the cultural and political domains on the other, or for that matter between economic stagnation or decline and the emergence of nations, as Walker Connor has conclusively demonstrated.[30]

This is not to deny that states and cultures have undergone radical changes, which parallel in intensity and depth those in the economic domain. But the nature of those changes, and the reasons for them, cannot be simply deduced from changes in the economic domain. They have to be discovered and analysed in their own right, for polities and cultures have characteristics and patterns of their own, which are quite different from those of economic systems. Nowhere is this more evident than in the sphere of nations and nationalisms.

2

The Modernist Fallacy

Perhaps the most common belief in the field holds that nations and nationalism are essentially phenomena of the nineteenth and early twentieth century, that before that century nations and nationalism were largely unknown and that economic and political developments which had been so conducive to their formation and proliferation are now, at the end of the second millennium, beginning to render them obsolete. Underlying these beliefs are certain assumptions about the nature of ethnic communities and nations.

These may be summarized as follows. First, nations and nationalism are regarded as inherently modern – in the sense of recent – phenomena; that is, they emerged in the last two hundred years, in the wake of the French Revolution. Second, nations and nationalisms are treated as the products of the specifically modern conditions of capitalism, industrialism, bureaucracy, mass communications and secularism. Third, nations are essentially recent constructs, and nationalisms are their modern cement, designed to meet the requirements of modernity. Finally, ethnic communities, or *ethnies*, to use a convenient French word, though much older and more widespread, are neither natural nor given in human history, but are mainly resources and instruments of elites and leaders in their struggles for power. Underlying these views, of course, is the fundamental assumption that modernity constitutes a revolution in human history, perhaps *the* revolution, one whose effects are ubiquitous and universal, and that all pre-modern eras are at an end and with them all the structures and beliefs that flourished and upheld those earlier, long-gone epochs. The past is, indeed, 'another country'.[1]

'Instrumentalist' approaches and 'primordial ties'

These are the basic assumptions which underlie what I shall call the 'modernist' and 'instrumentalist' viewpoints on ethnicity and nationalism, so prevalent today. First I shall say something about the instrumentalist approach.

Briefly, an 'instrumentalist' approach is one that regards human beings as having always lived and worked in a wide range of groups. As a result, people have a variety of collective identities, from the family and gender to class, religious and ethnic affiliations. Human beings are continually moving in and out of these collective identities. They choose, and construct, their identities according to the situations in which they find themselves. Hence, for instrumentalists, identity tends to be 'situational' rather than pervasive, and must be analysed as a property of individuals rather than of collectivities.[2]

To understand these views, we have to look on collective identities as so many resources and bounded categories upon which human beings can draw in different environments. Families, schools, congregations, classes, ethnic groups, genders, are all bounded units of resource upon which we, as individuals, can draw at different times and in varying circumstances. Their contents, and their meanings for us, are highly malleable. On the other hand, the social boundary between 'them' and 'us' is relatively permanent. The cultural contents and meanings of ethnic identities tend to change with cultures, periods, economic and political circumstances, according to the perceptions and attitudes of each member. They are never static, never fixed. It is vain to search for an 'essence' in such identities, because they are always being transformed and can always be refashioned according to need. Like Heraclitus' river, their forms and contents are always in flux, changing according to the current situation and the needs and preoccupations of groups and individuals. Only their social boundaries remain.[3]

Ethnic communities, or *ethnies*, are one such bounded resource, or rather set of resources, for individuals. Far from being rooted in human nature and history, not only is each *ethnie* different, each *ethnie* is constantly undergoing change. Being Italian or Russian today is not the same as in 1980, let alone 1960 – in the eyes of members of the group as well as outsiders. Nevertheless, ethnicity also provides a defined symbolic and organizational site for individuals and elites to mobilize resources in the pursuit of common goals within a state. Symbols, therefore, are important in shaping aggregates of resources (including people), in defining borders and giving members purpose and direction. Yet symbols, like every other cultural code, are variable and malleable; they can be adapted and even invented to suit group and individual interests and circumstances.[4]

In stark contrast to instrumentalist views stand those older attitudes to ethnicity which regard collective cultural identities, and especially *ethnies*, as having deeper roots within human society and history. There are various positions here, which are often included, summarily, under the generic label of 'primordialism'. The extreme version holds that we have an ethnic identity as we have speech, sight or smell. This form of primordialism regards human beings as belonging 'by nature' to fixed ethnic communities, in the same way that they belong to families. This is a common view among nationalists, though not all of them. We find it particularly in the 'organic' version of nationalism, which was first elaborated by early nineteenth-century German Romantics, but which can already be found among the followers of Rousseau in France. In this version, just as nations have 'natural frontiers', so they have a specific origin and place in nature, as well as a peculiar character, mission and destiny. In this view, no distinction is made between nations and *ethnies*. Both are seen as equally part of the natural order, and nationalism is a naturalistic attribute of humanity.[5]

A second version of primordialism is that associated with the recent revival of socio-biology. According to this viewpoint, *ethnies* and nations are 'natural', because they are extensions of kin groups which are selected by genetic evolution for their inclusive fitness – a view that received new impetus when the formulations of socio-biologists like Wilson, Trivers and Badcock were applied to ethnicity. Individual reproductive success is maximized by 'nepotism' as well as reciprocity, and cultural similarity is treated as an important means of guiding individuals in their quest for genetic reproduction through inclusive kin groups. The fact of biological origins of ethnic groups is reflected in their cultural myths of origin and descent. The work of Pierre van den Berghe is a succinct example of the application to ethnicity of the socio-biological revival.[6]

A third version of primordialism holds that ethnicity is in general a prior, given and powerful, indeed sometimes overwhelming or 'ineffable', social bond. But this emotional power is not inherent in the ethnic bond itself, it is felt by the participants in a given ethnic encounter or by the members of a particular *ethnie*. It is the members or participants that attribute a 'primordial' quality to their particular *ethnie*; in their eyes the ethnic tie has logical and temporal priority over other ties, and they acknowledge its compelling power and 'affect'. This does not mean that *ethnies* are fixed or static. On the contrary, historical ethnic communities form, flourish and dissolve, or are absorbed by neighbouring or conquering *ethnies*, even when their claims are fully recognized by their members. On this view, every human being must be a member of one or other ethnic community; ethnicity is essential to our understanding of history; ethnic bonds override other loyalties; yet given *ethnies* may lose their vitality, may fade and languish, to be revived by outside forces.[7]

The various versions of primordialism are open to a number of objections. The most obvious is that human beings live in a multiplicity of social groups, some of which are more significant and salient than others at various times. Hence the ethnic tie has no absolute priority. It is just one among a number of widespread but variable bonds that may bind human beings at given times. Second, ethnic ties like other social bonds are subject to economic, social and political forces, and therefore fluctuate and change according to circumstances. Moreover, frequent intermarriage and the importation of scarce skilled labour resulting from de-population caused by such factors as repeated urban epi-demics, extensive trading links with other areas and peoples, and the frequency of external conquests in history, have made it unlikely that more than a very small number of rather isolated *ethnies* ever possessed the cultural homogeneity and pure 'essence' posited by most primordialists (and national-ists). Third, as a result of these factors there is far more latitude for individuals to choose the ethnic community to which they prefer to belong, and so to shape their own and their family's destiny, than is allowed by primordialists; and this is particularly true of the late twentieth century.[8]

Besides, the mechanisms proposed by socio-biologists for explaining loyalties to much larger communities than fam-ilies, mechanisms like nepotism, projection and identifi-cation, are open to considerable uncertainty. It is not at all clear why the quest for individual reproductive success should move beyond the extended family to much wider cultural units like *ethnies* or how far a constant of this kind can help to explain the variable phenomenon of the modern nation. As for the more flexible versions of Geertz and Shils, they too suffer from a certain exaggeration of the *a priori*, affective and binding quality of ethnicity, and fail to see how ethnic choices are influenced by circumstances. In fact, ethnic solidarities are often the result of perfectly rational strategies of benefit-maximization on the part of individuals and groups, particularly in relation to significant others.[9]

There is a good deal of misunderstanding here. While some of the criticisms of the 'strong' (or naturalist) versions of primordialism are well taken, they overlook, or better explain away, the enduring and binding quality of many *ethnies* as well as their often dogged persistence over centuries, even when (perhaps because) they are part of wider polyethnic mosaics or hierarchies. They also overlook, or explain away, the powerful feelings of the participants or members of *ethnies* and nations concerning the collectivities in which they are involved. These feelings of belonging and obligation, of antiquity and dignity, the sense of a tie which is prior to and more powerful than other ties, are in and of themselves vital data for any investigation of the meanings of ethnicity. They cannot be dismissed because some of the primordialist explanations of them are inadequate or tautologous.[10]

More important, these criticisms confuse the individual with the collective levels. At the collective as opposed to the individual level, ethnicity remains a powerful, explosive and often durable force. Ethnic categorization and ethnic organization have been central to human association and conflict in most periods and continents. Many human beings have sensed the enduring power and hold of ethnic ties, and have often regarded their own *ethnie* as immemorial. Names, homelands, memories and symbols may linger on for centuries, despite the conquest, colonization or migration of the population they originally designated or delimited; this happened to the Punic culture long after Carthage had been destroyed by Rome, and again in Iran to the Persians when they were conquered by Muslim Arabs and Islamized from the seventh century on, yet retained their Persian name, homeland, myths and memories. In this sense, we may speak of a 'participants' primordialism', a sense of enduring ethnic ties among descendants of the original community, wherever they happened to be.[11]

The limitations of 'modernism'

I shall now turn to the parallel debate between what we may term the 'perennialists' and the 'modernists'.

This is an argument about nations rather than *ethnies* and ethnicity. For some scholars, nations too are perennial and immemorial. Their roots stretch back into the medieval era, or even antiquity. There never was an age without its nations and nationalisms, even if the doctrine of self-determination was born in the modern epoch. Every human being feels in 'his or her bones' the enduring power of their nation, the almost timeless quality of the national character. Nations can be found from earliest antiquity, from the beginnings of records in ancient Sumer and Egypt, and they have dominated political life in every era since that time.[12]

This is not a view that commends itself to the great majority of scholars. They subscribe to the rival modernist approach to nations and nationalism. According to this viewpoint, nations and nationalism are quite recent phenomena (usually dated to the time of the French Revolution, but sometimes to the Reformation), the product of the revolutionary modern forces of industrialism, capitalism, bureaucracy, mass communications and secularization. Some scholars combine this modernism with an emphasis on the constructed, even invented, quality of the nation as cultural artefact; and with a strong belief in the historically specific and transitory nature of nations and nationalism. For them, nations and nationalism are essentially nineteenth- and twentieth-century phenomena, tied to a particular epoch of 'modernity' which is gradually drawing to a close in the West, and whose obsolescence in advanced industrial societies, therefore, is beginning to become apparent at the end of the twentieth century.[13]

However, the modernist viewpoint is concerned less with the supersession of nationalism, than with its appropriateness or 'fit' with modernity. For modernists, both nations and nationalisms must be treated as intrinsic elements of modernity, and as inevitable components of the rise of the modern state. In one version, nations and nationalism are derived directly from the rise and nature of the modern territorial and professionalized state, first in the early modern West and then, through colonialism, in the annexed overseas territories in Latin America, Africa and Asia. It was the transformation of these monarchical sovereign states after the French Revolution through mass democratization and the spread of the ideal of popular sovereignty that brought the nation to prominence, and turned absolutist states into national ones. As we saw in the case of Hobsbawm's analysis, nationalism on this reading takes its force and meaning only from the conjunction of the nation with the modern state; and it is the state that determines the scope and power of any nationalism. At the same time, nations and nationalisms require external referents, and these are provided by a series of competing national states in a global interstate system.[14]

In a second version, nations and nationalism may be seen as a means of bridging the gap between state and civil society opened up in Europe since the Reformation, and the consequent alienation that this has engendered. Nationalism attempts to resolve the problem of state–society dissociation through a specious appeal to the idea of natural and historical culture-community, using arguments about authenticity and organic culture derived from Herder. In this way, it seeks to evoke a sense of organic community which masks the class conflicts and factions of modern societies in emotional appeals to solidarity. More recently, it has been argued that the reflexive nature of the state, with its monopoly of administrative, coercive and surveillance powers, and the exigencies of the interstate system, have formed the locus of nations and nationalism. The appeal to a culturally distinctive and sovereign popular community, in a modern era of dislocation, alienation and detraditionalization, complements and legitimates the powers of the modern state in a modern interstate system. Here then is the locus of violence and warfare. On this reading, nations and nationalism are inherent in a self-reflexive modernity that has today become truly global in scope and penetration. Moreover, new modes of distantiation of time and space and the 'disembedding' of many elements from their settings, so characteristic of modernity, have created a new desire for local units of trust and co-operation in the face of an alienating world. The nation represents one way of resolving these dialectical tensions created by modernity.[15]

Alternatively, nations and nationalisms are derived from the requirements of modern industrial social organization and its pressures for mass literacy and mobility. Unlike pre-modern polities and societies with their entrenched divisions between clerical and aristocratic elites and the mass of food-producers with their many local cultures, industrial society is a fluid, growth-orientated society; it derives its drive and legitimacy from its ability to fulfil material expectations. Such a society, whose material basis is industrial urbanism, is characterized by semantic rather than manual work. It has lost any anchorage in restricted and ascriptive role relationships and can only find its social solidarity in a particular kind of culture – a 'high' or 'garden' culture – either by turning 'low', spontaneous and oral cultures into cultivated, literate ones, or by forging the latter from the 'shreds and patches' of existing cultural materials, to accord with the needs of a fluid, egalitarian mass society. Only a modern growth-orientated society, capable of creating large-scale economic development, engenders the need for 'high' national cultures and the latter can only be sustained by state-directed and standardized, mass, public education systems.[16]

Modernist theories represent the dominant orthodoxy in the social scientific analysis of nations and nationalism. But there are several objections to all these modernist viewpoints. The first is historical. It is true that nationalism, the ideology and the movement, is a fairly recent phenomenon, dating from the late eighteenth century, but it is also possible to trace the growth of national sentiments which transcend ethnic ties back to the fifteenth and sixteenth centuries, if not earlier, in several states of Western Europe. Among their small clerical and bureaucratic classes, there are expressions of fervent attachment to the concept of the nation as a territorial-cultural and political community as far back as the fourteenth and fifteenth centuries in France, England, Scotland, Spain and Sweden, as well as in Poland and Russia and possibly Switzerland, if not Wales and Ireland. Certainly by the sixteenth century in England and the Netherlands, if not in France, a wider 'middle-class' nationalism of the urban educated began to take hold, one which elevated 'the people' to the sovereign position, a view soon to be reinforced by the myth of ethnic election encouraged by Puritan doctrines. These are the 'old, continuous nations' which Seton-Watson contrasted with the much later 'nations of design' created by and in the wake of nationalism.[17]

Sociologically, too, nation-building has proved elusive. Too often, the construction of nations has been equated with state-building. But state-building, though it may foster a strong nationalism (whether loyal or resistant to the state in question), is not to be confused with the forging of a national cultural and political identity among often culturally heterogenous populations. The establishment of incorporating state institutions is no guarantee of a population's cultural identification with the state, or of acceptance of the 'national myth' of the dominant *ethnie*; indeed, the invention of a broader, national mythology by the elites to bolster the state's legitimacy may leave significant segments of the population untouched or alienated. In many of the new states of

Africa and Asia, the assimilative power of the modernizing state has failed to prevent ethnic protest and disruption, let alone erode ethnic boundaries and cultures. In many cases from the Philippines and Sri Lanka to Iraq, Ethiopia and Angola, there has been not the fusion of *ethnies* through a territorial national identity but the persistence of deep cleavages and ethnic antagonisms that threaten the very existence of the state. In yet other cases, attempted fusion has been seen, often with reason, as ethnocide (if not genocide), and the victimized people or region has turned to mass resistance and protest, if not outright revolt and secession. This antagonism may stem from pre-state and pre-colonial ethnic relations, including ancient enmities, or alternatively from the social, economic or cultural effects of colonial 'modernization'. All this means that we should be wary of according too much weight to the powers of the modern state in our explanations of modern nations and nationalisms. There are other forces and factors which may predispose cultural populations and areas to the nationalist ideological programme.[18]

A third problem stems from the instrumentalism of most modernist theories. They have found it difficult to account for the dynamic, explosive, sometimes irrational, nature of ethno-national identity and ethnic nationalism in an increasingly interdependent world. Millions of men and women have sacrificed themselves, even their lives, for the fatherland, for 'la patrie', for France, for Italy, for Israel, for Vietnam. The instrumentalist approach to ethnicity, considered above, for all its recognition of the importance of symbols, fails to explain why people should choose ethnicity or nationalism as their vehicle of advancement rather than class or region. Why should so many millions of people respond to flags and anthems, national monuments and shrines, national festivals and commemorations? 'Rational choice' theory has sought to overcome this difficulty in terms of rational individualist strategies of maximizing public goods for the culturally defined population; but it still comes up against the uneven, explosive, angular quality of so much ethno-nationalism. Why should so many people be prepared to fight and die for ethnic communities whose struggles seem desperate and where any public good seems continually elusive? Why the readiness to become martyrs for minority causes that appear hopeless?[19]

This suggests a further gap in modernist and instrumentalist accounts. They concentrate, for the most part, on elite manipulation of 'the masses' rather than on the dynamics of mass mobilisation *per se*. This is the result of the 'top down' method employed by most modernist approaches. While the role of elites, notably the intelligentsia, is crucial, not enough attention is paid to the outlook and needs of the poor and powerless, nor to the ways in which their interests and needs are differentiated by class, gender, region and ethnicity. Nor has due weight been accorded to the ways in which each of these groups and strata can and have been mobilized in accordance with their own cultural and political traditions, their memories, myths, symbols and vernacular forms of expression. This is also true of those who, like Hobsbawm, recognize the importance of 'proto-national' communities and sentiments among the lower classes, yet refuse to connect them in any way with subsequent modern political nationalisms. Such a strategy debars us from grasping the popular power of nationalism, its capacity for mass mobilization, and the vital energizing role played by culture and symbolism.[20]

Perhaps most important, what I have called 'the myth of the modern nation' fails to grasp the continuing relevance and power of pre-modern ethnic ties and sentiments in providing a firm base for the nation-to-be. In their determination to show that all elements of 'tradition' have collapsed or been eroded by the revolutions of modernity, the modernists have failed to demonstrate that the global scope of those revolutions has been more marked in some areas than others, and has penetrated some strata and sectors more profoundly than others. Ethnicity and religion have, in fact, been two sectors that have resisted assimilation to the dominant secular and universalist ethos of modernity. This is even true in some of the Western heartlands of modernity. Though the political force of religion had greatly declined in the West (except Ireland, Spain and America), it is not accidental that the strong national states of Western Europe were built up around sizeable 'ethnic cores' (the English, the north-central French, the Castilians, the Swedes) which were able to incorporate, if not assimilate, their smaller neighbours into an enlarged national state, albeit with varying degrees of success. Outside the West, traditional and fundamentalist religions retain a powerful hold on millions of people. This is as true of the Indian subcontinent as of the Islamic lands. Similarly, today, many states outside the West have been able to forge nations where these have rested on the cultural base of a dominant *ethnie*. This is as true of some East European states (Poland, Romania, Greece) as of those new states in Asia (Thailand, Vietnam, Japan and Korea) which have had a long tradition of historic domination by a central strategic *ethnie*.[21]

In short, this myth of the modern nation has to be recognized for what it is: a semi-ideological account of nations and nationalism, one that chimes with modern preconceptions and needs, especially with those of a mobile, universalist intelligentsia, for whom the nation-state is only a staging-post in humanity's ascent to a global society and culture. It is as much a myth, in the sense of a widely believed and dramatized tale of a sacred past which serves present needs, as the myth of nationalism itself; and it should be treated with similar caution.[22]

Modernity and nationalism

There are also important empirical objections to modernist approaches.

For one thing, they overlook the era in which a given population begins its 'entry into modernity' by engaging in the cultural and political work of nation-formation. To have begun this project in, say, the early nineteenth century in Europe or Latin America, is quite a different kind of undertaking and leads to very different results from the nationalism and nation-building in Africa or Asia since the Second World War. The post-war era has witnessed a much more truly 'globalizing' setting of economic, technological and political interdependence than was imaginable, let alone realizable, nearly two centuries ago. Moreover, the difference in timing is important for the very different expressions of various nationalisms and the radically different types of nation that they help to create. The language and symbolism of the nation, if nothing else, are critically affected by the era in which they emerged, being more often than not influenced by one or more national centres – England, France, Russia, Japan, China – which acted as pioneers and models or recipes of national development.[23]

For another thing, modernist approaches critically undervalue the local cultural and social contexts. The latter are treated as so many 'local variations' illustrating the overall themes of nationalist modernization. But a moment's consideration will convince us of the misleading nature of such exercises. At best, the introduction of elements of 'modernity' may help to account for the timing of impulses towards nationalism or nation-formation. They tell us nothing about the character, intensity, durability or scope of the processes of nationalism. No doubt 'modernity' played its part in stimulating Aboriginal or Mohawk nationalisms in Australia and Canada, just as it had done in France or Russia; but how much does this tell us, even about the timing, let alone the scope and character, of these utterly different nationalisms which are otherwise 'worlds apart'?[24]

Equally important is the fact that nationalism continues to flourish, if in sometimes less violent forms, yet with much vigour and tenacity, in some of the most advanced industrial societies – in France, Canada (Quebec), Catalonia and the United States. This again suggests that cultural movements like ethnic nationalism are relatively independent of the processes of modernity and it raises important problems for modernization theories of nationalism.

In France, with its tradition of revolutions, where an advanced economy, a highly centralized state and professionalized bureaucracy, and a well-educated and relatively affluent population exemplify the features of a fully modernized society at the heart of the global economy, ideologies have come and gone, but nationalism and a powerful sense of national identity remain constant and potent. Negatively, this was expressed in French objections in the 1950s to the European Defence Community, France's Gaullist opposition in the 1960s and 1970s to NATO and American hegemony, its opposition to American cultural demands in the Uruguay round of the GATT discussions, and the antipathy entertained by many French men and women in the 1970s, 1980s and 1990s towards Muslim immigrants, towards Jews and towards 'les Anglo-Saxons' and their cultural hegemony. Positively, these feelings were matched by an equally fervent passion for France's rich cultural and ecological heritage, a powerful attachment to her historical traditions, an ardent love of the French language, a keen sense of her historic frontiers, a visible pride in the symbols of French glory and in her accomplishments from architecture and literature to cuisine and cinema. And all this despite the strong regionalism which France still displays, and the many doubts and criticisms levelled in recent years at the received national traditions in history textbooks, in the art-history canon, in museology and various other fields. Gaullism and its concept of a 'Europe des Patries' was only one political expression of this underlying cultural nationalism which roots the French state in French culture and society.[25]

In Quebec, too, there is a relatively wealthy, advanced industrial society which is part of a wider North American globalizing economy, displaying all the hallmarks of a fervent nationalism which teeters on the brink of 'sovereignty-association' while pursuing the goal of complete cultural independence. One might have expected that, after the 'quiet revolution' of the 1960s and the successful transfer of much of the professional and business activities of the province to Francophones, the Quebecois would have contented themselves with the assurance of French cultural hegemony and provincial 'home rule'. But this has not proved to be the case. French Quebecois sentiments and ideologies have remained vibrant, and powerful, forces in the political life of the province, provoking ethnic and national counter-forces from the other provinces of the Canadian federation. Indeed, there are fears that, after the collapse of the Meech Lake Accord and the new powers of the Quebecois opposition party in the Federal Parliament, a new movement of secession on the part of one of its wealthiest ethnic components could finally force through the breakup of the Canadian state.[26]

Catalonia has, from the late nineteenth century, been one of the most successful commercial and industrial regions of Spain, with Barcelona becoming a leading entrepôt and a major European centre of culture. Its cultural nationalism was born of the mid-nineteenth-century literary and cultural *Renaixenca* and flourished in many literary, cultural, artistic and scientific movements, academies, journals and parties at the turn of the century. Since then, Catalonia has been among the most economically and culturally advanced regions of Europe and after a long popular resistance to the cultural oppression of Franco's regime, it has once again emerged as a strong centre of ethnic nationalism, winning a large measure of political autonomy from Madrid. Despite (perhaps because of) its thorough modernization, Catalonia remains a nation with a strong sense of its historic national identity and passionate aspirations for maximum autonomy in the Iberian peninsula.[27]

In the United States of America itself, the most dynamic arena of modernization, a powerful continental providential nationalism is not hard to mobilize. Every time United States soldiers are killed or captured in a UN mission, every time the President agonizes over a foreign-policy issue involving an American military presence, every time trade negotiations threaten to favour America's competitors, the sense of a separate and unique American history and destiny looms in the background, encouraging Americans to feel their common historical mission as the bearers of freedom and democracy. This shared patriotism, this messianic belief in America, this quasi-religious sense of a common destiny, seems to be independent of the economic and political vicissitudes of the United States or of American society, for it emerges in every kind of context and it does not seem to wane with growing affluence and mass high consumption. The belief in an American Creed, Constitution and way of life, overarching the many cultures of its constituent *ethnies*, has remained a resilient force, despite the many setbacks and disappointments of Americans at home and abroad.[28]

In other less developed but rapidly modernizing societies like Poland, Norway and Ireland, ethnic nationalism remains a powerful force, and the sense of common nationality is deeply ingrained and widely diffused in the population. It is fed, of course, by fear of common enemies – in the Polish case by fear of the former Soviet Union, in the Norwegian case by anxiety about the impact, economic, political and cultural, of a European Community led by Germany and France, and in Ireland by historic suspicion of England – but it springs also from the historical legacy of separate statehood and/or incorporation as a marginalized, even submerged and oppressed community in a larger, more advanced state. While it is possible to interpret the vivid expressions of nationalism in these countries as legacies and survivals from a previous, nationalist, era, the fact that they recur and are still widely diffused suggests that it is necessary to look more closely at the social and ethnic origins of these collective sentiments and aspirations.[29]

There is also the more recent phenomenon of rabid xenophobia and ethnic violence directed against immigrants, *Gastarbeiter* and asylum-seekers. This takes popular as well as official forms. At the popular level, the last few years have seen virulent outbreaks of anti-Semitism in Germany, France, Poland, Hungary and elsewhere, together with even more violent hatreds directed at Turkish, Albanian, Gypsy and other immigrants or *Gastarbeiter* in Germany, Italy, France and the Czech Republic. These have been inflamed by various neo-fascist or neo-Nazi organizations, claiming under the banner of patriotism to defend the purity of the national cultural heritage and received national identities, as well as to safeguard job opportunities for natives. At the official level, both national and Pan-European policies against asylum-seekers and immigrants have been coordinated by European governments and rules of entry have been tightened, at the very moment when the Single European Act and the Maastricht Treaty have unified the native European populations of the European Union, allowing them free entry and mobility throughout the territories of the union. Here too is striking evidence of the paradox of unification and fragmentation, and of the difficulty of squaring the recent resurgence of ethnic nationalism with any idea of modernization as a painful transition whose successful crossing into the realm of democratic mass affluence is rewarded by national harmony and social peace.[30]

Identity, continuity and transformation

The continuing power of ethnicity, and the persistence of ethnic nationalisms even in advanced industrial societies, constitutes a major stumbling-block for myths of the transcendence of ethnicity through modernization as well as for recent modernist theories of nations and nationalism. The main reason for this failure is their refusal to link the consequences of modernity with an understanding of the continuing role played by cultural ties and ethnic identities which originated in pre-modern epochs. These ties and identities are found among local and regional communities, that is, among the lower strata – the peasants, tribesmen, artisans, labourers – which have often formed the social bases of mass-mobilizing vernacular nationalisms. This failure has meant a systematic neglect of the popular base and cultural framework of nationalism. To provide a realistic account of the paradox of fragmenting nationalisms amid global transcendence, this analysis must start with this popular base and its ethnic past, with the memories, myths, symbols and traditions of cultural communities. The critique of the fashionable modernist approaches to nationalism provides a necessary starting-point for a better understanding of recent political and social trends.

Any attempt to grasp the post-modern trends of transcendent eclectic globalism and the new localism must, therefore, relate them not merely to processes of modernization, but also to earlier pre-modern identities and legacies that continue to form the bedrock of many modern nations and exert a powerful influence today. Medieval France and Russia form not merely the basis, the crucible, of modern France and Russia; the social relations and cultural practices of the latter are embedded in the traditions, myths, memories, symbols and values that have been handed down from generation to generation, exerting to this day a powerful, if sometimes hidden, influence – in political traditions, in law and customs, in the landscape and its sacred places, in language and literature, architectural forms, artistic and musical legacies, dances, costumes, food and recreations of the people. This means that the continuities with pre-modern influences must be analysed in conjunction with modern and 'post-modern' trends and their interrelations revealed, if the current proliferation of cultural identities and ethno-nationalisms in every part of the world is to be explained.[31]

I conclude with an example of what I have in mind. Even small and neutral national states like Switzerland, which have for so long resisted the temptations of being drawn into European political alliances and rivalries, are now feeling the pull of mass communications, transnational companies and markets, and of European political unification. So much so that even the 700th anniversary celebrations of Switzerland's political foundation myth in 1991 were somewhat muted; the country's problems, particularly for its youth, seemed to have little to do with the heroic founding era, or with the simple, sturdy virtues associated with Swiss independence. Today these problems appear to be either local or global, rather than simply national, and the old pedagogical national narrative which was so prevalent in Switzerland until the 1970s, seems less and less relevant.

Yet hardly two decades have passed since Switzerland was rocked by a campaign to keep foreign, mainly Italian, workers out and preserve Swiss jobs for the Swiss and keep the purity of Swiss political culture and the country's lifestyles intact. This meant preserving the sovereignty of the national state which had been founded in 1848 (or in the earlier Helvetic Republic of 1798) and which had lasted well into the 1970s. Behind that insistence on Swiss political independence stood a much longer history in which the Old Swiss Confederation had defended its cantonal rights and political cultures against a series of external enemies, a long-drawn-out process in which the community had been forged through struggle and by separation of a growing Swiss identity from those of its great neighbours.[32]

Here three broad epochs of Swiss continuity and transformation may be discerned. First, there was a long, pre-modern era of ethnic formation, when the various cantons were loosely, often ambivalently, brought together on the basis of Alemannic valley traditions and urban institutions, and the common fight to preserve or win back local privileges eroded by the Habsburgs. This was later seen as a heroic era, associated with various foundation legends (Oath of the Rutli, William Tell), and framed by external conflicts with Habsburgs and Burgundians. Only from the sixteenth century did non-Alemannic, French-speaking cantons and cities seek to join the Confederation, forcing the Swiss to seek other, non-linguistic bases for their political identity. This was followed by a period of consolidation on the basis of urban patriciates and interlocking oligarchies.[33]

When that identity threatened to ossify in the eighteenth century, a movement of cultural and political renewal in Zurich, Berne and Geneva led to the welcoming of French influence and intervention. This opened a second, modern epoch of ideological nationalism and nation-formation, in which various secular elites attempted to spread the ideas of a national Swiss identity to their countrymen. It culminated in the establishment of the Swiss Federation and the 1848 Constitution following the brief religious war of 1847 and the institutionalization of a modern national state.[34]

Finally, there is the gradual opening out of a neutralist, defensive Swiss national state and political culture to outside economic and political influences, which began in the 1960s but has since accelerated. It is as yet too early to say where this 'post-modern' phase will lead and whether it may erode the Swiss polity or Swiss political culture and identity. The point, however, is that we cannot begin to gauge this possibility without taking fully into account the whole length of previous Swiss history and identities, at least as a starting-point for subsequent analysis.[35]

This is a point both about substance and about method. Substantively, any new mode of Swiss identification will be informed by memories, symbols and traditions of earlier identities. This is inevitable, even if some younger urban

Swiss may wish to reject the older identities. Either way, any new European identity among the Swiss youth is likely to be permeated by older Swiss identities. Methodologically, any deeper analysis of changes in collective Swiss identification must accord due weight to these older identities which have guided the majority of Swiss men and women for so many centuries. Any new modes of Swiss identification will, in the long run, owe as much to older Swiss identities as to recent European and global trends. On both levels, the Swiss example provides a helpful guide for understanding the nature of the paradox and for grasping the significance of modern ethnic nationalisms which have recently experienced so marked and widespread a resurgence.

3

An Ethno-National Revival?

The failure of the modernist viewpoint to account for the resurgence of nationalism throws our original paradox into sharper relief. As we have seen, the revolution of modernity has by no means exhausted itself. At the same time, ethnic fragmentation and separatist nationalism are fundamental trends in recent history, not some temporary by-play, and they persist even in areas of advanced modernity. So why should they be renewed with such force at a time when the trends of modernity and the erosion of traditional values seem to contradict the particularism and fragmentation which ethnic nationalism continually engenders? What can an ethnic revival signify in the late twentieth century? Why have the fires of ferocious nationalism been rekindled, not forty years after they were thought to have burnt themselves out in the *Götterdämmerung* of the Third Reich?

The critique of perennialism

Or is it a rekindling and a revival? Perhaps we have been deluded: the fires of nationalism were never quenched, only temporarily screened from view by our guilty realization of their awful consequences. Even in the West, ethnic nationalism survived under a thin veneer of social democracy and liberalism. Many of the post-war movements for ethnic autonomy which surfaced in Europe in the late 1950s and 1960s can be traced back much earlier. The movements for Breton and Flemish autonomy were founded immediately after the First World War, the movement for Scots autonomy emerged in 1886 and the Scottish National Party's predecessor in 1928, the Basque movement of Sabino Arana was founded in 1894, and the Catalan movement in the 1880s.[1]

Although these and other Western movements experienced a mass renewal in the 1960s, their cultural origins can be traced as far back as the early nineteenth century and their early political manifestations to the late nineteenth century. Only the revulsion against racism and everything connected with ethnicity induced by the horrors of the Second World War can have obscured the persistence of these ethnic nationalisms from view and occasioned such surprise at their apparent sudden renewal.[2]

But dates do not tell the whole story. What exactly survived, what was revived? Was there a popular nationalism in the nineteenth century, which was revived in the 1960s? Can we speak of an ethnic community surviving intact from even earlier, pre-modern times? Or was there a pre-modern 'nation' that had, as the nationalists would have it, 'fallen asleep', to be revived 'with a kiss' in the heady atmosphere of the swinging sixties?[3]

This is very much the standpoint of the 'perennialists'. From their viewpoint, modern nations are simply recent examples of an age-old phenomenon, the immemorial nation, instances of which can readily be found in antiquity and the Middle Ages. There is nothing really new about the 'modern' nation, except the period in which it emerges and the technology and apparatus which its administrative and military elites can command. The nation as such, which they see as a named community of shared culture, history and language in its own homeland, has hardly changed. What we are witnessing in the late twentieth century is merely a reassertion of the national 'base' over the political and economic 'superstructure', to reverse (as nationalists themselves are wont to do) the Marxist metaphor. In other words, culture, national culture, has reasserted its primacy over politics, economics and technology, for culture is the unchanging fabric of society, with its slow rhythms of communication, its deep structures in the human psyche and its all-encompassing symbolic codes and networks of social relations.[4]

But, can the idea of the 'immemorial nation' be upheld? Can we maintain that the nation has, in some sense, always 'been there', the same in antiquity as in the modern epoch? Can we realistically claim that modern nations are the lineal descendants of their medieval counterparts, that the modern Russian or English nations are in all essentials identical with medieval Russia and England, or that these communities were the 'true ancestors' of the modern English (or Russians), as the introduction to the exhibition catalogue on the Anglo-Saxons *The Making of England* put it?[5]

Such a view suggests that 'modernity', for all its technological and economic progress, has not affected the basic structures of human association and that, on the contrary, it is the nation and nationalism that in each case leads us towards or brings about what we call 'modernity', each nation defining that modernity in its own way. Thus the ancient Jewish commonwealth under the Hasmoneans (Maccabees) and Herodians, for example, boasted the same features of homeland and people, history, language, central cult, as well as kingship, army and capital as many of their neighbours; and several of these are the same features that we find in modern nations. Is it not possible that the concept and reality of the nation is, after all, perennial, and that it determines our view of history, including what we call the modern era, and all its works?[6]

Now it is, of course, possible always so to define the concept of the nation that it will be coextensive with every larger territorial and cultural identity in any epoch. In that sense, the nation cannot be distinguished from the ethnic community or indeed from any collective cultural identity and community. Nevertheless, as a general viewpoint, perennialism is flawed. It makes some sweeping assumptions about the underlying nature of cultural communities, overlooks some important differences between pre-modern and modern culture-communities and oversimplifies an often complex picture of human association. To begin with, modern nations are 'mass nations'. That is to say, they appeal to the whole people and when they elevate the 'people' into the nation, they theoretically include all strata of the designated population in the sovereign nation – even if it took several centuries for this claim to be realized fully in practice, with the emancipation of women in the early twentieth century. Parallels in antiquity or the medieval era are rare – the ancient Jews constitute perhaps a significant exception. The mass nation, when it emerges, is in important respects different from the small elite groupings that usually pass for 'nations' in antiquity and the Middle Ages and which generally included only the upper strata. In the modern 'mass nation', every individual member is a citizen and there is theoretical equality of citizens in the community. The laws of the nation apply equally to all citizens and in theory there are no intermediate bodies mediating between citizens and the national state. This means also that the citizenry of mass nations is generally much more numerous than the politically active membership of pre-modern *ethnies* or city-states.[7]

In the second place, the modern nation is a 'legal-political' community, as well as a historical culture-community. There are two aspects here. The first is internal. The modern nation is a community governed by common codes of law and membership in such a community is therefore a legal as well as a social status. A citizen is understood as one who, in virtue of sharing in the common public culture of the nation, exercises certain rights and performs certain duties towards his or her co-citizens. These rights and duties are laid down in formal constitutions or in common law, or both, but the underlying assumption is that the latter are codifications of the national will which expresses the shared pattern of values and traditions of the community. The external aspect of modern nations is revealed in the concepts of autonomy and sovereignty. The modern nation is a 'political community' in its exercise of self-government and autonomy in relation to other nations, either within a federation of nations or as a sovereign national state among other sovereigns. It is a national political community insofar as it requires government to be national self-government of the whole community.[8]

In the third place, modern nations are legitimated through a universally applicable ideology, nationalism. As an ideology, nationalism holds that the world is divided into nations, each of which has its own character and destiny; that an individual's first loyalty is to his or her nation; that the nation is the source of all political power; that to be free and fulfilled, the individual must belong to a nation; that each nation must express its authentic nature by being autonomous; and that a world of peace and justice can only be built on autonomous nations. This 'core doctrine' of nationalist ideology emerged only in the eighteenth century, first in Europe and then elsewhere, although some of its components were foreshadowed in the sixteenth and seventeenth centuries. It was unknown before 1500 in Europe or elsewhere, and therefore anything resembling the modern mass nation (underpinned by nationalism) was likely to be fortuitous as well as rare. Modern nations implicitly subscribe to this nationalist ideology, and frequently invoke elements of it to underpin various claims and practices.[9]

Fourth, the modern nation is part and parcel of a wider international system, one in which the whole world is divided into separate national states which are then related to each other by common ideas and practices, including those implicit in the nationalist ideology. This system came into being in Europe after the Treaty of Westphalia in 1648 and became the dominant pattern in Europe, North America and Latin America after 1815. It was then carried by colonialism and the post-colonial state-nations to other parts of the world – to the Middle East, Asia and Africa. As I shall argue later, the dominant principles of the modern world are cultural and political pluralism. They ensure that the national state is the norm of both government and interstate relations, and that popular consent is the only theoretical justification for the tenure of political power.[10]

Finally, the modern nation is pre-eminently territorial in character. That is to say, the nation is a human population that is territorially bounded with mobility throughout that territory and whose members belong to a particular territory which is recognized as 'theirs' by right. There is a close correspondence, even union, between the homeland and its resources and the people, one that is mediated through history as seen through the eyes of the participants and often of neighbours. The people and the land are united both through a shared landscape and the ecological base of a unified economy and as a result of a history of shared experiences and memories, of common joys and sufferings, which tie events to specific places – fields of battle, scenes of treaties, habitations of princes, retreats of saints, colleges of sages and so on. It is by the banks of these rivers, on those hills and mountains, in these valleys, that 'our people' were born, were nurtured and flourish; the landscapes of the nation define and characterize the identity of its people.[11]

These are some of the characteristics that underlie the concept of the nation in the modern world. They suggest a working definition that unites territorial, legal and public cultural elements with the shared memories and heritage that characterize any collective cultural identity. On this reading, a nation can be defined as 'a named human population which shares myths and memories, a mass public culture, a designated homeland, economic unity and equal rights and duties for all members'.[12]

But, as this working definition suggests, we have sketched in only part of the picture. True, we may not find 'nations' in pre-modern epochs, at least not in the mass, legal, public and territorial form they took in recent centuries. On the other hand, we do find a number of looser collective cultural units, which we may call *ethnies*, and which we can define as 'named units of population with common ancestry myths and historical memories, elements of shared culture, some link with a historic territory and some measure of solidarity, at least among their elites'. These cultural collectivities, or *ethnies*, which I have discussed elsewhere, have appeared in the historical record since at least the late third millennium, since the ancient Sumerians, Elamites and Egyptians, and they have reappeared in every continent at different periods of history.[13]

If nations are modern, at least as mass phenomena legitimated by nationalist ideology, they owe much of their present form and character to pre-existing ethnic ties which stemmed from earlier *ethnies* in the relevant area. Of course, many earlier *ethnies* disappeared, or were absorbed by others or dissolved into separate parts; examples include the Phoenicians and Assyrians in antiquity, and the Wends and Burgundians in the medieval era. Nevertheless, some ethnic ties have survived from pre-modern periods, among at least some segments of given populations, and these have often become the bases for the formation of latterday nations and nationalist movements. The modern Breton movement clearly relies for its appeal on the persistence of Breton traditions, myths, memories and symbols, which survived in various forms throughout the long period of metropolitan French domination from the incorporation of Brittany through dynastic alliance in 1532. Similarly, Catalan nationalism, which emerged in the 1880s and experienced a revival in the 1930s and again in the 1970s, has drawn for its inspiration on the long maritime history of Catalonia, when it was a powerful semi-independent kingdom, and on the attraction and prestige of the Catalan language and culture. Croat and Serb nationalisms today resume earlier periods of popular nationalism, both in the mid-twentieth and in the nineteenth centuries, which are themselves dependent on modern reworkings of popular memories and symbols of independent medieval kingdoms and of ancient religious differences.[14]

This is not the place to explore further the possibility of pre-modern nations. What is clear is that, while some recent Western nationalisms hark back to nineteenth-century popular nationalisms, their forms and goals are significantly different today; and while in pre-modern epochs, we encounter many *ethnies* and several ethnic states, the evidence for pre-modern nations is at best debateable and problematic.[15]

Pre-modern ethnies

The preceding discussion has made it clear that, if we are to grasp the import of any 'ethnic revival' and resurgence of nationalism in the contemporary world, the sources of the power of these political forces must be traced back to the 'ethnic substratum' of collective identity and community. This requires a brief recapitulation of the main concepts used in the analysis of pre-modern *ethnies*, to enable us to locate the different routes by which they have given rise to modern nations.

'Lateral' and 'vertical' *ethnies*

Pre-modern eras are characterized by various kinds of ethnic community in different areas. The most common have been the 'lateral' or aristocratic, and the 'vertical' or demotic types of *ethnies*. 'Lateral' *ethnies* are fairly extensive and diffuse in character, but their ethnic culture is confined to the upper classes – the Court and bureaucracy, clergy, nobility and rich merchants. Hence the *ethnie* is also a high-status group. 'Vertical' *ethnies* are territorially more compact. Their ethnic culture spreads to all classes of the community and barriers to entry tend to be high. Their members, too, can be more easily mobilized by ethno-religious movements of renewal and by charismatic leaders, who often emerge from 'the common people'. Both types of *ethnie* may at times be fired by a sense of mission and myths of ethnic election – Hungarian knights and Catalan nobility as much as Arab or Israelite tribes, Swiss peasant warriors or Sikh militants. In each of these cases, we can trace the persistence of various collective vernacular memories, myths, traditions, rituals and symbols. Both among lateral and vertical *ethnies* they help to forge and preserve a historical culture-community, distinguished by specific work patterns and life-styles. Many of these culture-communities have persisted for generations, with the vertical or demotic *ethnies* often frozen, as it were, into a composite mosaic of (usually subordinated) status groups, despite undergoing many changes. The result is that in the modern era they form varying degrees of ready-made or 'available' networks of interaction and sentiment, endowing population clusters with a sense of familial intimacy and separate ancestral identity, in contrast to the 'alien' ways and beliefs of outsiders.[16]

The modern era is, from this standpoint, no *tabula rasa*. On the contrary, it emerges out of the complex social and ethnic formations of earlier epochs, and the different kinds of *ethnie*, which modern forces transform, but never obliterate. The modern era in this respect resembles a palimpsest on which are recorded experiences and identities of different epochs and a variety of ethnic formations, the earlier influencing and being modified by the later, to produce the composite type of collective cultural unit which we call 'the nation'. As we shall see, the differences and conflict between the two basic forms of *ethnie*, the lateral and the vertical, will be found to underlie many of the political problems and conflicts of the contemporary world.

The situation is similar with regard to the movement and ideology of nationalism. Of course, no such secular ideology or movement is recorded before the eighteenth century – or in religious form, before the sixteenth century in the Netherlands and England. But there were earlier ideologies and movements which prefigured nationalism. These are ethnicist movements in defence of given *ethnies*, both lateral and vertical, and an ethnocentrism whose basis is a missionary sense of ethnic chosenness. Sometimes such movements flared up into open revolt and warfare, as when the Ionians and Egyptians revolted against the Achaemenid Persians, the Gauls and Jews against the Romans, and the Swiss and Scots against the Habsburgs and Plantagenets. These ideals and the heroic legends that grew up around these exploits have undoubtedly influenced the modern nationalist aspirations of particular *ethnies*; and a later, secular nationalism has modified but retained some of the older heroic traditions and myths of ethnic election.[17]

'Core' and 'periphery'

A second important ethnic legacy from pre-modern epochs has been the survival of many so-called 'peripheral' *ethnies*. These are usually demotic or 'vertical' in character. Examples from the West would include the Quebecois, Basques, Catalans, Corsicans, Bretons, Welsh, Scots, Frisians, to name just a few; outside Europe, there are the Ewe, Bakongo, Copts, Kurds, Druse, Sikhs, Nagas, Tamils, Moro and Australian Aborigines. These ethnic communities have in the past stood (and in some cases still stand) in relations of alienation and subordination to larger, dominant *ethnies* whose elites ruled the state into which they had centuries ago been incorporated by expansionist lords and monarchs, or more recently by European colonial powers. The leaders of these peripheral *ethnies*, or the leaders of movements claiming to speak on their behalf, frequently contend that their communities continue to be exploited and oppressed in varying degrees. In the past, social, cultural and political issues formed the basis of protest. Today economic issues predominate, with the peripheral communities claiming their resources and labour are exploited and their regions are neglected or marginalized by governments dominated by the core or strategic *ethnie* in the state.[18]

There are a number of aspects to this situation. First, as noted before, modern Western states have been built up on the basis of 'core' *ethnies* – Castilians, French, English, Swedes – whose elites and monarchs forged strong states which then incorporated surrounding minority populations. A similar principle applied in other areas of Europe, though with less success: in Russia, Poland, Hungary and Yugoslavia. In the Eastern European cases, there was a dominant *ethnie* around which the state was constructed – Russians, Lithuanians, Poles, Magyars, Serbs – but the territory of the state included a number of significant 'peripheral' *ethnies*: Ukrainians and Tatars, Jews, Gypsies, Croats, Muslims, etc. This 'mosaic' of dominant-and-subordinate, centre-and-periphery ethnic relations has formed the historical background to the rise of the national state in much of Europe, but it can also be found outside.[19]

Second, in relation to a given state and its dominant *ethnie*, the incorporated ethnic communities and categories were treated as sociological minorities. That is to say, they were not only minorities in numerical terms, they were also marginalized and discriminated against, in varying degrees. The French slogan: 'No Breton, no spitting', can stand for the many prejudices against ethnic minorities that stemmed from their subordinate status. As Michael Hechter has documented for the industrialized West, such minorities were subject to a whole series of economic exploitations, social exclusions and cultural discriminations. Their economies were distorted to suit the market and commodity needs of dominant *ethnies*, their skilled labour was often forced to emigrate, their elites were culturally assimilated, high status positions were reserved for members of the dominant *ethnie*, social welfare for minority communities was restricted, and there was a much higher rate of social alienation among minorities – more crime, more alcoholism, higher divorce rates and the like.[20]

Third, these ethnic minorities retained into the modern epoch a sense of their cultural distinctiveness. They remained, in varying degrees, separate from the culture of the state and of the dominant *ethnie*. This could result as much from their 'frozen' subordinate status as from any penetration of trade and capitalism. We find ethnic communities retaining a sense of their separateness in 'backward' agrarian states as well as in 'advanced' industrial ones, among relatively illiterate communities as much as in culturally well-equipped states. This applies not just to diaspora *ethnies* like the Armenians, Greeks, Jews and Gypsies, but equally to resident *ethnies* like the Basques, Slovenes, Czechs, Ukrainians, Finns, Tatars, Kurds and Tamils, and latterly to communities as distant and culturally diverse as the Mohawks in Canada, the Uigurs of China and the Aborigines of Australia. In all these cases, some traditions, values and symbols that distinguished the minority from the culture of the dominant *ethnie* and the state, retained their hold on segments of the population.[21]

Uneven ethno-history

It is, however, another feature of the pre-modern legacy that was to have the most profound consequences once the processes of modernization began to affect different areas of the world. This was the uneven diffusion of ethno-history.

By 'ethno-history' I mean not an objective historian's dispassionate enquiry into the past but the subjective view of later generations of a given cultural unit of population of the experience of their real or presumed forebears. That view is inseparable from what the historian and social scientist would term 'myth'. As intimated earlier, 'myth' does not signify fabrication or pure fiction; generally speaking, myths – particularly political myths – contain kernels of historical fact, around which there grow up accretions of exaggeration, idealization, distortion and allegory. Political myths are stories told, and widely believed, about the heroic past that serve some collective need in the present and future. Ethno-history, or ethnic *mythistoire*, in turn represents an amalgam of selective historical truth and idealization, with varying degrees of documented fact and political myth, stressing elements of romance, heroism and the unique, to present a stirring and emotionally intimate portrait of the community's history, constructed by, and seen from the standpoint of, successive generations of community members.[22]

Ethno-history is characteristic of most cultural communities in all ages, whereas scholarly, dispassionate history is a minority phenomenon peculiar to certain societies and civilizations. The Homeric poems and the Bible are among the most familiar examples in the Western tradition of ethno-historical writing; the epic and the chronicle have always been the main forms of pre-modern ethno-history. This kind of didactic history has other characteristics: an emphasis on the heroic and dignified, a belief in the example of virtue, a story of the origins and early wanderings of the community, perhaps also of liberation from oppression and unification, an account of the foundation of the polity, above all a myth of the golden age of warriors, saints and sages, which provides an inner standard for the community, an *exemplum virtutis* for subsequent emulation, and a spur and model for ethnic regeneration. Greeks could look back to classical Athens or Justinian's Byzantium, Romans to the early republican era of Cincinnatus and Cato, Jews to the kingdom of David and Solomon or the times of the Sages, Arabs to the Age of the Companions, Persians to the Sassanid epoch, Indians to the Vedic era and Chinese to the classical age of Confucius.[23]

Now such ethno-histories are not equally distributed among the world's populations. On the contrary, some communities are well endowed with rich, and fully documented, ethno-histories, while others are bereft of their ethnic pasts, and have few records of their ancestors' experiences and activities. On the whole, the major *ethnies* have been able, by dint mainly of political monopoly, to retain and preserve their ethnic heritage, and especially their ethno-histories. They have full records, rich and diverse memories, well-developed codes of communication, institutional record-keeping and a class of specialists in the creation, preservation and transmission of such records, usually priests and scribes but also bards, prophets and artists. Many of the smaller, demotic and peripheral *ethnies*, on the other hand, excluded from the instruments of political transmission and bereft of institutional support, and sometimes without a class of specialists and developed codes of communication, have been unable to salvage much of their ethno-histories beyond a few generations. Their memories are tenuous, their heroes shadowy, and their traditions, if not entangled with those of other, more powerful neighbours, are patchy and poorly documented.[24]

To this a rider must be added: some *ethnies*, because of their strong alternative modes of transmission (usually through decentralized or itinerant religious and cultural personnel), have been able to preserve and transmit their heritages and ethno-histories from generation to generation – one thinks of diaspora peoples like the Jews and Armenians, but also of oppressed resident *ethnies* like the Irish, Basques, Kurds and Sikhs.[25]

Reappropriating one's culture

The uneven diffusion of ethno-history has exerted a strong influence on the course of nationalist mass mobilization, which continues right into our era of advanced modernity. We can distinguish a number of overlapping cultural phases of a process in which vertical, demotic *ethnies* are turned into ethnic nations. At the outset, tiny nuclei of indigenous intellectuals, exposed to the cultures of more advanced states and experiencing a crisis of legitimate authority, become fired by a desire to rediscover their community's ethnic past, and begin to realize the extent or lack of knowledge of that history and to compare it with the known traditions, myths and shared memories of other communities. We might term this the first stage of historical reappropriation. Historians, linguists and writers attempt to rediscover the community's past and to elaborate, codify, systematize and streamline into a single coherent ethno-history the various collective memories, myths and traditions that have been handed down piecemeal from generation to generation. Where there is a well-established ethno-history in a canonical form, they select and use those of its components which in their judgement can serve specific political purposes.

Through these activities, first the intellectuals, then the wider stratum of professionals or intelligentsia, and finally other classes, are brought back to their real or presumed indigenous traditions and customs, languages and symbols, myths and memories, many of which are still extant in one form or another among the peasantry or in certain provinces that are deemed to retain an authentic tradition. This was the case with a number of French intellectuals and artists who made the pilgrimage to Brittany with its ancient, religious and hence 'authentic' culture. Such was also the case with the province of Karelia in Finland, where Elias Lönnrot, Akseli Gallen-Kalela and other Finnish artists and intellectuals repaired to rediscover an authentic and heroic past, which they took to be the remaining exemplar of Finland's ancient history, embodied in its peasant ballads which Lönnrot wove into the Finnish epic, the *Kalevala*.[26]

The recovery of an ancient ethno-history, then, is the starting-point for the subsequent process of vernacular mobilization. It is essential for any nationalist aspirations to be satisfied, that the chosen community be furnished with an adequate and authentic past. This is why the concept of 'authenticity' is so important. It attests to the originality, the self-generating nature, of a given culture-community. Since Anthony Ashley Cooper, 3rd Earl of Shaftesbury, popularized the idea of the genius of a nation, and since Herder's advocacy of the idea of the original and authentic spirit of a nation, authenticity has become the litmus test for any cultural, and hence political, claims. To say that an *ethnie* lacks an authentic culture and ethno-history is to deny its claim to national recognition.[27]

But authenticity and dignity are the hallmarks of every aspect of ethnic culture, not just its ethno-history. Of these the best known and most important is language, since it so clearly marks off those who speak it from those who cannot and because it evokes a sense of immediate expressive intimacy among its speakers. The outstanding role played by philologists, grammarians and lexicographers in so many nationalisms indicates the importance so often attached to language as an authentic symbolic code embodying the unique inner experiences of the *ethnie*. Though language is not the only significant aspect of the nation, as so many Central and Eastern European nationalists claimed, and as the experience of so many Asian and African nationalisms appears to have contradicted, it remains a vital symbolic realm of authentication and vernacular mobilization.[28]

The process of vernacular mobilization extends into other realms – to the arts of music, dance, film, painting, sculpture and architecture, to the national appropriation of landscapes, historical monuments and museums, and to the construction of a national political symbolism and mythology. Visual art and music have been of special importance in the crystallization of authentic national imagery and its dissemination to a wider audience. The popular reception accorded to certain ethnic and 'nationalist' paintings by David and Delacroix, Mihály Muncasy and Akseli Gallen-Kallela, Vasili Surikov and Diego Rivera, to Eisenstein's or Kurosawa's ethno-historical films, to the operas of Verdi, Wagner and Musorgsky, or the symphonies and symphonic poems of Elgar, Dvořák and Tchaikovsky – or in this century, of Bartók, Janáček and Sibelius – reveal the growing mobilization of wider social groups into the vernacular ethnic culture reappropriated and sponsored by native intellectuals.[29]

The 'vernacularization' of political symbolism is particularly important for demonstrating the irreplaceability of ethnic culture values in a global moral economy. For the nationalists, certain events and heroes, and certain signs, are elevated into national icons. It might be the figure of a Caesar or a King Alfred, an era like the golden age of Athens or the kingdom of David and Solomon, a monument like Great Zimbabwe or Angkor Wat, or a rejuvenated tradition like Emperor worship in Meiji Japan. Or it might be a mythology of national revolution, or of refoundation, like the celebration of Bastille Day in France or the Fourth of July in the United States of America – or the Great Trek and the Battle of Blood River celebrated annually by the Afrikaners. All these efforts are prompted by the need to demonstrate the possession of a unique, authentic and adequate cultural heritage and ethnic past, one which will bear comparison with those of other nations. The fact that nationalist intellectuals must, so often, labour to furnish the community with these culture values is evidence for their very uneven diffusion, and for the burning desire in many communities to compensate for a perceived deficiency of ethno-history and ethnic culture.[30]

Cultural politicization and purification

The next phase of national regeneration moves into the political arena. It involves two processes, the politicization of culture and the purification of the community.

As outlined above, certain symbols, events, heroes and monuments of the past were endowed with new national meanings. Moses, for example, was traditionally for the Jews the 'Master of the Prophets' and God's greatest servant. For Zionists, however, he became a national hero, a liberator of his people, a national lawgiver and leader. Likewise, Muhammad in Islamic tradition is Allah's greatest Prophet and his message the final revelation, but for Arab nationalists he has become primarily a national leader of the Arabs, the founder of the Arab Islamic nation, and the greatest expression of an Arab national genius. Whole eras of the past may be similarly politicized, and their meanings transformed by a 'retrospective nationalism'. So the post-Vedic era of classical Indian city-states became the golden age of Aryan India, and Arjuna a prototype of the fearless patriot; and the pagan era of Cuchulain, Fin Mac Coil and the High Kings of Tara in fourth-century Ireland was now invested with heroic grandeur and became a golden age of Irish national glory.[31]

Not just the past, but also the folk culture of the present can take on a political aspect. Polish, Swiss or Hungarian peasant customs and institutions have become models for national life-styles and the national regeneration of an effete cosmopolitan urban class. This kind of ethnic populism, with its cultivation of peasant customs, traditions, sports and crafts, has become almost inseparable from the pursuit of national ideals. It was greatly assisted by movements of political romanticism that mobilized the intelligentsia and other strata from the early nineteenth century. For romantics, the arts, literature, architecture, crafts, song and dance, dress and food, were all imbued with the creative, yearning spirit of the people, and demonstrated their native genius. Only by rejoining the people through their vernacular culture, could latterday urban classes 'realize' themselves in their uncorrupted, authentic being.[32]

The politicization of native culture, therefore, often went hand in hand with the purification of the community. This meant, first of all, jettisoning all 'alien' cultural traits – words, customs, dress, food, artistic styles – and reappropriating vernacular traits for a renewed indigenous culture. But it also meant purifying the people themselves, forging the 'new man' and the 'new woman', in the image of a pristine ideal found only in an idealized past of heroic splendour. Thus 'volkisch' writers of the nineteenth century held up the vision of the old-German colonist, a settler on virgin soil, living a pure and simple life in nature. In the same way, Slavophile writers in nineteenth-century Russia idealized the old, classless, pre-Petrine Russia and its sacred union of Church, land and people under their redeemer-Tsar.[33]

To purify the community entailed a hardening of attitudes to foreign elements and ethnic minorities in one's midst. Where before minorities and foreigners had been tolerated as millets or middleman trading enclaves, they now came to be seen not just as economic rivals, but as indigestible cultural elements, or, worse, as insidiously eroding the moral fibre and biological purity of the nation. The desire to preserve intact the unique cultural heritage of the people was soon transformed into anxiety over the threat to the destiny of the community, a sense of impending national decline and thence into a fanatical hatred of everything alien. This in turn led to the branding of ethnic minorities, who had long lived side by side with each other or with majorities, albeit sometimes uneasily, as an imminent danger to the very existence and character of the nation, to be surgically removed, where possible.

So the desire to create a homogenous moral community worthy of its heroic ancestors and regenerated through its politicized, vernacular culture required the purification of its citizenry and the rigorous exclusion, or destruction, of everything alien. The history of Codreanu's Legion of the Archangel Michael is a good example of this progression. Starting as a movement of romantic nationalist populism against urban values and bourgeois capitalism, it preached the defence of the native culture and the Romanian country-side against the depredations of urban cosmopolitanism. But it soon degenerated into a vigorous and brutal proto-fascism, which sought the purification of the Romanian community through a militant crusade of violence against Jews and foreigners.[34]

Today, too, we can still witness the incipient desire to purify a reborn community in Eastern Europe and Russia. Small but vociferous movements of national regeneration urge the radical purification of the liberated nations of the East through the exclusion of their foreign elements, and once again anti-Semitism follows hard on the heels of a romantic conservative nationalism. Movements like *Pamyat* (memory) in Russia or *Vatra Romaneasca* in Romania use ethno-religious metaphors – of mother Russia, of Russia as a holy monastery, of the chosen Slavic people, of the Romanian hearth and home – to kindle in their followers the ideal of a purified community contaminated by foreign, and especially Jewish, cosmopolitan elements. Not until they have been removed can Russia (or Romania) resume their destinies and mission as the truly chosen Orthodox Slavic community.[35]

In milder form, the appeal to vernacular culture, the politicization of that culture and the desire to purify the community have left their mark on the movements for ethnic autonomy in the West from the 1960s on. Few of these movements have drawn the full logical consequences of their ideals in the manner of East European movements before the war and recently. But the same desire to rejuvenate a neglected culture and community informs the Scots, Welsh, Breton, Basque, Catalan and Occitanian movements.[36]

In all these movements, there is the same logic of vernacular mobilization, cultural politicization and communal purification. The Breton movement sought to re-create through folksong and the arts a cultural revival, in opposition to a pervasive French cultural influence; the Welsh Language Society has tried to rejuvenate the Welsh language and keep the dominant English influences and people at bay; Basques have striven from time to time to exclude foreign elements and Castilian intrusions using racial ideas. In each case, though in varying degrees, there has been concern for a dying language, fear of ethnic and cultural admixture and decline, anxiety over the loss of traditional life-styles, and a sometimes violent desire to mobilize the populace against the dominant ethnic power, the French, English and Castilians.[37]

The social background of neo-nationalisms

It may be objected to this that recent ethnic nationalisms, particularly the Western movements, do not really fit the cultural pattern that I have outlined here, and that we would do better to search for their roots and character in recent economic and social trends.

The theoretical reason for my having said little about the economic aspects of ethnic nationalisms should be clear. 'Modernist' theories generally emphasize social and economic causes, implying that nations and nationalism are products of the large-scale social changes associated with the rise of capitalism. The present analysis departs from such a 'modernist' standpoint, arguing instead that modern nations and nationalism are grounded in pre-existing ethnic ties and their political mobilization, and are formed by this legacy, a view which inevitably accords a lesser role to purely economic factors. It would be absurd to claim that socio-economic causes like capitalism, urbanization and industrialism are irrelevant to the birth and course of nationalism, or that they do not play a significant role in the creation of ethnic conflicts and the treatment of ethnic minorities. But the assumption that ethnic conflict and nationalism can be ascribed to predominantly economic factors appears equally one-sided. Besides omitting the crucial domain of politics, such a view suggests that recent ethnic nationalisms can be largely understood without reference to the historic cultural and social components of ethnic categorization and identification, a claim that is both inherently implausible and empirically unconvincing. In the case of Western ethnic neo-nationalisms, socio-economic factors may help to explain the social composition of such movements, but they tell us little about their character, forms and intensities, or why they emerged among some of Europe's peripheral *ethnies*, and not others. Economic factors do not help us to answer the question of why it was Basques and Bretons, rather than Sicilians or Frisians, who sought ethnic autonomy.

We can pursue this a little further by considering the familiar arguments about ethnic labour markets. This holds that most modern ethnic conflicts are ultimately reducible to social antagonisms resulting from competition over labour markets in a capitalist society. Either capitalists attempt directly to divide the labour force on the lines of ethnic categories through unequal wages, or the exploited workers themselves seek to better their wages, security and working conditions by policies of ethnic discrimination and job reservation. Similarly, white-collar professionals and other middle strata may seek to restrict to their own ethnic kinsmen the opportunities for jobs and education in a competitive market.[38]

It suffices here to say that such arguments have force only to the extent that they implicitly accept both the fact and the shared significance of ethnic categorization and identification. It would be pointless to attempt to divide along ethnic lines a labour force whose cultural characteristics were, and were perceived to be, homogenous. Nor would it prove possible to restrict job opportunities to ethnic kinsmen, if a sense of ethnic identity and difference was lacking in the population of a given state. In one sense, this is a truism. But, in another sense, it points to the nature and independence of ethnic variables in any social setting: to the importance of myths of common ancestry, historical memories and a shared culture, and of attachments to land and people. It is just these characteristics that constitute the pervasive legacy of premodern *ethnies* in the modern world.

My claim is not that economic factors play little part in the genesis and course of ethnic neo-nationalisms. Clearly, they do, if only in the form of catalysts. Economic trends or crises often account for the timing of ethnic nationalisms. But, as Walker Connor has convincingly shown, ethnic nationalisms can emerge in every kind of economic setting – advanced, backward, improving, declining and stagnant. Ethnic nationalisms do not generally correlate with economic trends.[39]

Rather the contribution of long-term economic trends to the creation of nations and nationalism should be viewed in the context of class formation and wider class roles. These trends apply equally to capitalist and state socialist societies, since nations and ethnic nationalisms figure prominently in both socio-economic formations. Economic variables form the background for the formation of those classes and strata which have habitually taken the lead in ethno-nationalist movements in both kinds of economy, notably the mainly secular intelligentsia, from whom such movements have derived much of their impetus. *Their* needs, preoccupations and aspirations have tended to dictate the goals and strategies of ethnic nationalisms, in community after community. Though the significance of this stratum has varied between societies, it has been at the forefront of nationalist movements all over the world.[40]

This is especially true of recent ethnic nationalisms in both West and East. In the 1960s and 1970s a new more technical intelligentsia, supported by businessmen and traders, spearheaded the protests against the centralized Western national state, both in North America and Europe, to be followed in the late 1980s and 1990s by their counterparts in Eastern Europe and the former Soviet Union. To take the West, first. In Quebec, for example, professionals of all kinds – lawyers, doctors, journalists, teachers, engineers, pharmacists, technicians and the like – pushed through what came to be known as the 'quiet revolution' of the early 1960s. They wrested power in the province from the traditional leaders of an agrarian and Church-dominated community, and began to agitate for the recognition of the French language in all walks of life and for its parity with English. The return to the vernacular in modern life was accompanied by a movement for the elevation of Francophones into middle-class positions and, in the shape of the *Parti Quebecois*, for their assumption of political power in the province. From here it was a short step to the demand for full ethnic autonomy, and ultimately ethnic secession.[41]

In the United Kingdom, the movements for greater ethnic autonomy have been led by a growing intelligentsia, notably in Scotland. There the Scottish National Party, supported predominantly by professionals and small businessmen, has striven for outright independence since at least the 1960s. Yet, though on the face of it the economic climate has been favourable, with the discovery of North Sea oil, most Scots have failed to respond to this appeal, especially in the devolution vote of 1979 which fell well short of the 40 per cent requirement – though thereafter autonomy and devolution have again become political issues. These political variations seem unrelated to the strong and persistent popular consciousness of a Scottish national cultural identity and an overall desire for greater autonomy. While the majority of Scots seem to want more local participation, the process of Scottish political mobilization has been limited by the long tradition of Scottish involvement in a wider British society and polity, and by the strong hold of the Labour Party in Scotland. The flexibility of the British state over the decades has also damped down separatist demands, at least until recently, as has the ability of Scotland to make its political voice sufficiently heard in both local government and the law, and through national institutions like the Scottish Office.[42]

In Wales, this process of vernacular mobilization has had less success. Despite the efforts of intellectuals in the Welsh Language Society, the Welsh language is largely confined to the agrarian north of the country; the industrial south has opted for an English-language Welsh identity, saturated with strong working-class traditions. Despite the retention of a distinctive Welsh culture, manifested in the preference for chapel over church, in the traditions of poetry, choral singing and sports, and in the cultivation of collective historical memories in the *Eisteddfodau* and *Gorsedd*, support for the Welsh Party (*Plaid Cymry*) remains low, and the influence of English society and the British state is marked. The impact of a Welsh nationalist intelligentsia has been limited, though at least two of the Welsh colleges (Bangor and Aberystwyth) conform to the well-known pattern of nationalist fervour found among university staff and students.[43]

In Catalonia, too, the influence of the Catalan language and the Catalan intellectuals has been pervasive. This is traceable to the mid-nineteenth century literary *Renaixenca* (mentioned in chapter 2 above) and to the cultural and political nationalism of influential figures like Prat de la Riba in the early twentieth century. Franco's repression of Catalan culture and language had the effect of broadening and deepening the influence of both, since resistance naturally centred on their protection in the private domain. Since the transition to democracy, there has been a strong revival of Catalan culture and Catalan language publications, coupled with increasing demands for maximum autonomy, many of which have been conceded in the form of a revived ethno-regional institution of self-government.[44]

In these cases, ethnic agitation for greater autonomy by a native secular intelligentsia has been limited both by the historic presence of a wider political identity and by the possibility for democratic accommodation of ethnic grievances. On the one hand, the long-term incorporation of peripheral *ethnies* and the interventionist power of the central state of the hegemonic *ethnie* has added another circle of political identity and loyalty to the original ethno-national one; Bretons, Scots and Catalans can and do also feel French, British and Spanish, particularly to outsiders and abroad. At the collective level, the historic central national state has been able to forge its own political national identity on the basis of territory, law, citizenship and political culture, usually over centuries – even though at first this was unintended and only dimly perceived.

On the other hand, the growth of democratic institutions and practices has helped, in varying degrees, to counteract the alienation of peripheral ethnic populations and their intelligentsias. They have been able to provide channels through which their collective grievances might be redressed and their interests accommodated. While no Western poly-ethnic state can be said to have 'solved' its underlying ethnic problems, those states with a long democratic tradition have so far been able to alleviate ethnic grievances, forge an inclusive political mythology and symbolism and shape a system of common values and political memories for all their constituent *ethnies*. They have also generally had the wealth and political (often imperial and colonial) power to offer high-status positions to ambitious, educated members of the peripheral *ethnies*. Examples that spring to mind include the Corsicans in France and Scots in the British Empire.[45]

Intellectuals, ethnic myths and religion

While the secular intelligentsia play an important part in popular Western ethnic neo-nationalisms, their recent role in

Eastern Europe and the former Soviet Union has been pivotal. Here the leadership of an even smaller stratum of 'pure' or 'free-floating' intellectuals has been widely acknowledged. This recalls the well-known distinction of Hans Kohn, who argued that, unlike 'Western' nationalisms with their rational and civic character and bourgeois social base, the nationalisms of 'the East' (east of the Rhine) owed their often authoritarian, mystical and 'organic' character to the leadership of a small stratum of intellectuals in the absence of a bourgeoisie. This, of course, is to simplify matters; intellectuals have been crucial in French and English nationalism, which are unimaginable without Rousseau and Michelet, Milton and Burke. There is, however, some truth in the linkage for the more recent era, since the command economy of soviet-style communism vacated the social and political space of discontent and alienation to a dissident intelligentsia, who were encouraged to link their concerns for human rights with ethnic and national grievances by the recent heavy-handed communist policies in both areas.[46]

Intellectuals of this 'organic' kind have played important roles in Western neo-nationalisms as well; Hugh McDiarmid in Scotland, Saunders Lewis in Wales, Yann Fouere in Brittany, Frederico Krutwig among the Basques, have prepared and articulated the ethnic renascences of their respective communities and proposed strategies for their realization. But in the East, intellectuals and professionals have been even more prominent in nationalist politics. The role of the intellectuals in popular movements like the Prague Spring and the Czech Velvet Revolution of 1989, the Croat movement of the early 1970s and the Polish Solidarity movement is well known. Equally vital has been their contribution to *Sajudis*, the Lithuanian national movement, and to *Rukh*, the Ukrainian national democratic movement; many of the leaders, including the first president of an independent Lithuania, were intellectuals. The intelligentsia have also been prominent in the growth of a populist Russian nationalism, and intellectuals have played a leading role in the post-

1967 growth of dissident refusenik Jewish nationalism in Russia. Indeed, one of the most pressing problems confronting the Soviet Union in its death throes was the growing demand by republican and other ethnic intelligentsias for greater political power, a demand that could not ultimately be accommodated within the existing Union, or be reconciled with the claims of the many Russian settler communities in non-Russian republics.[47]

With the breakdown of the universalism of Marxist communism, first into a polycentric national communism and thence into ethnic nationalism, the intellectuals and professionals were driven back to their respective ethnic heritages and mythologies, in the hope of realizing the messianic promise of a revolutionary transformation of society within their own communities. But theirs has been a disappointed universalism, transposed onto a limited, infertile terrain, of the kind that Eduard Shevardnadze has encountered in his native Georgia and Leonid Kravchuk, communist-turned-nationalist, in the Ukraine. In other cases, resistance to communism was fuelled by a long-suppressed nationalism. In Poland, Solidarity had close links with a national Catholic Church as well as with nationalist Polish intellectuals, and successive Polish governments have placed a national Polish interest at the centre of their concerns and policies.[48]

In the Czechoslovakia of the late 1980s, Vaclav Havel and his Civic Forum merged their concerns for human rights with a steadfast national solidarity in the face of a Russian-backed soviet-style regime. But, beneath the surface, the tensions between the poorer Catholic regions of Slovakia and the more advanced and Westernized Czech society – tensions that had found clear expression in their different regimes and statuses during the Second World War – injected a strong note of ethnic nationalism into the aftermath of the Velvet Revolution, preparing the way for the peaceful dissolution of Czechoslovakia. It may not be possible to trace with ease the

recent parting of the ways to the different cultural back-
grounds, histories and linguistic traditions of the Czech and
Slovak *ethnies* and their homelands, and the uses to which
they have been put by elites on both sides. But the uneven
depth and distribution of their respective ethno-histories, the
former peripheral status and overshadowing of the Slovaks
by their culturally better equipped neighbours, and the
Slovaks' desire to assert their national individuality, form the
cultural substratum, basic parameters and historical
legitimations of recent political movements and actions.[49]

The role of such ethnic memories, myths and symbols, and
their uses by intellectuals and other elites, have been the
subject of considerable debate in accounting for recent conflicts in Eastern Europe and the former Soviet Union. Few
would dispute the centrality of intellectuals and professionals
in the leadership of many ethnic nationalisms in these
countries, but their role is viewed in quite different terms by
instrumentalists and primordialists. The former see the intellectuals as fashioning and orchestrating national conflicts
through their manipulation of ethnic memories, symbols and
myths; their pursuit of rational strategies based on their
economic and status interests largely determines the shape
and content of so many ethnic nationalisms in Eastern
Europe, the Balkans and the former Soviet Union. This is
especially true of the former Yugoslavia: Franjo Tudjman the
historian confronts Radovan Karadžić the poet, but both
construe and fashion the symbols and goals of the conflict
they have done so much to guide for their own partisan ends.
Primordialists, on the other hand, are inclined to minimize
the role of elites, including intellectuals, and to trace the
sources of the Serbo-Croat conflict to underlying historic
antagonisms of which the intellectuals are merely the
articulators and executors. In this view, deep religious differences and historic conflicts going back to the medieval epoch,
as well as the very different trajectories of Serbs and Croats
under the Ottoman and Habsburg empires, have produced

the collective antipathies so brutally manifested in the mass-acres of the Second World War and again today.[50]

Neither position seems adequate to explain the complexities of these conflicts. Serbo-Croat hatred (and brotherhood) are in fact fairly recent, going back to the 1920s at the earliest, when they were first incorporated into a single Serb-dominated Yugoslav kingdom; before that time, despite the intellectuals' dream of south Slav unity in the early nineteenth century Illyrian movement, the two peoples had separate political traditions and histories, and were separated by rival empires. On the other hand, the political manipulations of Serb and Croat intellectuals could become effective only where sufficient members of their ethnically designated constituencies were ready to respond to the call of ethnicity and the content of its myths, memories and symbols. Moreover, if religion is today more a 'badge' of ethnicity than a profound spiritual force in the former Yugoslavia, its political potency derives from centuries of cultural differences and social exclusion between Serbs, Croats and latterly Muslims which have become part of the fabric of society in the Balkans. What remains, and what can and has been used to such devastating effect, is a rich harvest of symbols, memories, myths and traditions in which epics of battles, legends of sages and saints, and ballads of heroes and bandits, are handed down from generation to generation as living cultural traditions of the people in the small towns and villages. It is in the intellectual and popular uses, and limits, of these fundamental symbolic components of ethnicity that we must search for more adequate answers to the variations of inter-ethnic relations and the invocation of nationalism as the ultimate political and territorial solution to ethnic relations in mixed areas.[51]

The role of intellectuals and professionals must therefore be placed within this longer historical setting and broader cultural context. The pivot of this analysis can be neither the aims and activities of the intellectual, professional and other elites, nor the mass sentiments and memories of the common people, but the often complex relationships between the two. In the social and political role of the intelligentsia we see a microcosm of our initial paradox: the well-known 'crisis of identity' which afflicts so many educated men and women, as they move from a more restricted and traditional form of society to one that is more open, mobile and pluralistic, mirrors the contradictions of the wider society. The education of the modernizing intellectuals and professionals, with its culture of critical discourse, and its universalistic rational and technical ethos, binds them to their counterparts in every land. On the other hand, by separating them from their ethnic kinsmen, from 'the people', professional rationalism sets up countervailing emotional and cultural pressures of alienation that can only be resolved by a new type of identity and community, one based on vernacular mobilization and the reappropriation of authentic history: that of the modern nation, an autonomous political community in which intellectuals and professionals may apply their skills and training, but in the service of the people, their ethnic and civic compatriots.[52]

This process of reappropriating an ethnic past has also helped to foster a powerful religious revival. The return of many secular Muslims in Bosnia to Islam, the growth of strong Islamic movements among the Islamic communities of the West and the vigorous, sometimes fanatical, espousal of Islam and Hinduism on the Indian subcontinent, even the return to nationalist Orthodoxy in Russia, are all related to the intensification of ethnic ties and a sense of ethnic election among embattled ethnic communities in what they feel to be an alien, if not hostile, environment. This is coupled with a deep ambivalence over the values of modernity. On the one hand, the technological, economic and military power associated with Western modernity commands respect, even emulation; on the other hand, there is a deep revulsion against what appears to be the social and moral breakdown engendered by unregulated rationalism and unbridled progress. This revulsion quickly takes on religious and ethnic dimensions. 'The West' or 'Western Christianity' is categorized as the Other in relation to which 'the pure', 'the noble' and 'the elect' must realize their true worth and find redemption. This means rejecting the anomie of 'Western values' in favour of the retention of traditional family structures and ethnic values, ancient customs and communal faiths. It is, however, through their ethnic exemplifications that the Islamic, Hindu, Orthodox, Jewish and Buddhist revivals become politically effective: in Iran, Syria and Algeria, in India, Russia and Israel, in Sri Lanka, Burma and Tibet. This is true even of the Shi'a revolution which threatened to engulf the Middle East. Its roots and growth in Iran ensured a strong influence of Iranian nationalism over the political expressions and activities of Shi'a Muslim revolutionaries – as well as of Iranian clerics and centres of learning.[53]

Herein lies a particularly acute contradiction. The spread of global patterns of politics and communications have helped to revive the ethnic ties of many communities through the return by many people to religion and religious mythologies, particularly in India, the Middle East and Africa. But this is not simply a collective response of fear and protest against the pressures of globalization in its Western forms. This revival is to be found in some Western and Westernised heartlands of modernity, too: in America, the Netherlands and Japan, as well as in Israel, Poland, Ireland and Mexico. The Protestant revival and the renascence of Catholicism and Judaism, though not as impressive as the resurgence of Islam or Hinduism, have considerable followings, and are often linked to ethnic self-assertion and myths of ethnic election. In such cases, religious mythologies act as guarantors of the redemption of oppressed *ethnies* or reinstators of by-passed ethnic values and life-styles. Through the myths of the resurgent religion and its chosen bearers, the forces of modernity can be brought under control and made to serve the interests of aspirant or marginalised classes and *ethnies*.[54]

Conclusion

Hence, it is a mistake to see in the return to radical forms of religion an expression only of fear and resentment, or of the collapse of traditional values and symbols. The global picture is more complex. Given the community-forming propensity of most religious myths, symbols and traditions and the longevity and pervasiveness of their influence, there is nothing unexpected or remarkable in a return by either the elites or the wider populace to such traditions and symbolic systems to see how they can help, and make sense of, both the opportunities and the tribulations of rapid change and modernity. Above all, the return to religion and its myths of ethnic chosenness enables elites and people alike to relativize their immediate experience through traditions that continue to promise the salvation of immortality beyond the present order of experience. At the same time, they increasingly combine this traditional promise with an expectation of terrestrial redemption in the collective afterlife for the chosen through the judgement of posterity, that is, the judgement of one's descendants who form the next generations of an identical community of history and destiny.

What is happening, then, in so many areas of the world is a double collective appropriation: of the traditional message of individual and collective salvation beyond the world of experience, and of the new nationalist message of collective immortality for the elect through posterity and its judgements. The union of these two appropriations is the singular achievement of the historicist vision of humanity and the premium this places on the unique culture values and destiny of each historical segment of humanity. It is the achievement of nationalism to have given political expression to these twin

---

83

appropriations by linking the memories of ethno-history and the older religious myths of election to the striving for collective territorial recognition and political autonomy in a historic 'homeland'. In the modern world, such autonomy and recognition are best secured and preserved in a state of one's own.

4

The Crisis of the National State

When people assert that the nation-state has had it day and that other forms of political association have become more appropriate vehicles of post-modern or post-industrial processes and trends, they are making a number of separate claims. The first, as explained above, is that global communications and economic trends transcend national boundaries and that the nation-state can therefore no longer maintain its control over these and other processes. This claim was refuted in chapter 1. A second, related, claim, also touched on, is that there is a zero-sum relationship between national and other forms of political association and that the new forms of political association necessarily involve the relegation of nation-states as foci of political loyalty. To this claim I intend to return in chapter 5.

Here I want to consider a third claim: that contemporary nation-states are undergoing erosion, if not disintegration, because their plural, or polyethnic, character is undermined by the processes of state expansion and modernization and by the problems they have engendered.

Bureaucratic incorporation

It is both true, and significant, that most modern states are plural. In that respect, they are clearly not nation-states. At best they are 'national states'.

Strictly speaking, we may term a state a 'nation-state' only if and when a single ethnic and cultural population inhabits the boundaries of a state, and the boundaries of that state are coextensive with the boundaries of that ethnic and cultural population. (This, of course, is a criterion which would rule out ethnically homogenous states some of whose co-ethnic and co-cultural population inhabit neighbouring, or indeed other, states.) In this sense, there are very few nation-states. Portugal, Iceland, Japan (except for the Ainu and Koreans), Denmark (except for the Faroese), are examples. Several states, like Poland, have come to approximate this model. Nevertheless, less than 10 per cent of all states in the United Nations are nation-states. Most states are polyethnic in character and many are severely divided along ethnic lines, some of them with numerically significant ethnic minorities and others divided into two or more large *ethnies* – such as Burma, Indonesia, Malaysia, Kenya, Nigeria, Belgium Canada and Britain.[1]

How did this state of affairs come about? Nations, as I indicated, were formed along two main routes. The first that I discussed was through a process of vernacular mobilization and it has accounted for a large percentage of today's national states. The second route was essentially a process of bureaucratic incorporation. This began from the base-line of 'lateral' *ethnies* – extensive, ragged in boundaries, and largely confined to the upper strata. In most cases, in fact, an aristocracy led usually by a king or prince and his court and staff, and supported by the clergy, ruled over one or more regional or ethnic communities and categories who supplied the labour and services necessary for the maintenance of the aristocracy's life-style. This was the pattern in much of

Europe, and it persisted in the eastern half of the continent after the three great empires – the Habsburg, Romanov and Ottoman – were fully established. It also persisted well into the nineteenth century in other parts of the world – in the Middle East, in South Asia and the Horn of Africa. In the course of the nineteenth century, the European colonial empires established a modified version of this basic pattern; in this case, the 'aristocracy' in question was an overseas administrative elite, sometimes supported by missionaries and settlers, forming a 'parallel society', a pattern already established in Central and Latin America in the sixteenth century.[2]

These 'lateral' or aristocratic *ethnies* were generally content with preserving the basic pattern of cultural difference and political hierarchy. This was true of the many ancient ruling aristocracies such as the Hittites, the Medes and Persians, and the Philistines, who made little or no attempt to incorporate members of subordinate *ethnies*, at least on any scale, into their dominant culture and society. Content to receive tribute, labour or services, the elites of the dominant *ethnie* happily preserved the cultural gulf between themselves and the ethnic categories and communities whom they had conquered and whose lands they had annexed and were exploiting.[3]

But, for reasons that remain not altogether clear, a few of these aristocratic or lateral *ethnies*, or their rulers and clergy, began to feel the need to spread their ethnic culture donwards and outwards – to some of the middle (if not lower) strata and to some of the outlying regions of their domains. In both cases, defence considerations may have played a crucial role. Constant attacks by marauders and other states may have prompted a firmer policy of cultural incorporation in the marchlands of the aristocratic state, such as occurred on the Welsh borders, in Languedoc and Provence or in Finland. This was often achieved by settling ethnic kinsmen on the volatile frontiers, or by a greater measure of central administrative control, or both. Ecclesiastical control could also be used to this end: recognition of the jurisdiction of the higher clergy over the disputed or ethnically mixed lands helped to secure them for the aristocratic state. Religion may also have supplied a motive. In the Spanish case, the defence of Catholicism against Muslim invasion became a fundamental component of later Spanish national identity, while in the French case, Papal backing for Frankish and later Capetian claims for ethnic 'chosenness' in defending the Catholic domain proved crucial for the later expansion of French royal jurisdiction, especially in the face of the heretical tendencies in Languedoc. Much later, religion was used by English Tudor monarchs not only to bolster their own position in England, but also to prevent continental Catholic powers from attacking England through Ireland by extending English control in Ireland through Protestant settlements.[4]

Certainly, it was in Western Europe that the processes of bureaucratic incorporation of outlying regions and middle strata became most evident. Broadly speaking, the absolutist monarchs increasingly sought to standardize and homogenize their ethnic populations. At first, this was a by-product of their need to increase their revenues and military resources to maximize their effectiveness in the competition between dynastic states which became the dominant element in European politics from the late fifteenth century. In the mid-sixteenth century the debilitating political effects of religious strife within kingdoms following the Reformation hastened the process of homogenization. By the seventeenth century religious and cultural standardization and homogenization were increasingly seen as a precondition of success in inter-state rivalries, Richelieu's measures of linguistic reform and Louis XIV's Revocation of the Edict of Nantes being only the most obvious examples. A century later England's leadership was being attributed to its early political, linguistic and religious unity and the ensuing ideology of liberty.[5]

The processes of bureaucratic incorporation have been various. They include the familiar measures of state-making:

creation of a single code of law and system of courts throughout the territory, creation of a single taxation system and fiscal policy, construction of a unified transport and communications system, streamlining of the administrative apparatus and centralization of control in the hands of the ruler in the capital city, formation of professional cadres of skilled personnel for the key administrative institutions, and the creation of effective military institutions and technology under central control. At a later stage, measures of welfare benefit, labour protection, insurance, health and education came to be included in the processes of state-making; and these were usually accompanied or succeeded by an extension of the franchise to middle and then lower strata, and finally to women.[6]

Alongside these processes of state-making there developed a strong national consciousness. This was partly the result of the state-making processes, but it was also the product, and later also the cause, of overlapping if analytically separable processes of 'nation-building'. This is a term often used interchangeably with state-making processes, but the foci and emphases of nation-building processes are rather different.

They include:

- the growth, cultivation and transmission of common memories, myths and symbols of the community;
- the growth, selection and transmission of historical traditions and rituals of community;
- the designation, cultivation and transmission of 'authentic' elements of shared culture (language, customs, religion, etc.) of the 'people';
- the inculcation of 'authentic' values, knowledge and attitudes in the designated population through standardized methods and institutions;
- the demarcation, cultivation and transmission of symbols and myths of a historic territory, or homeland;

- the selection and husbanding of skills and resources within the demarcated territory;
- and the definition of common rights and duties for all the members of the designated community.

The emphasis throughout these processes is subjective: these are mainly attitudes, perceptions and emotions connected with symbols, myths, memories, traditions, rituals, values and rights. But they also involve definite sets of 'objective' activity: the authentication, cultivation, selection, designation, preservation and inculcation of values, symbols, memories and the like. These processes of nation-building also tie in with our working definition of the nation as 'a named human population which shares myths and memories, a mass public culture, a designated homeland, economic unity and equal rights and duties for all members'.[7]

State penetration and the crisis of legitimacy

During the nineteenth and twentieth centuries, however, there has been an enormous increase in the power and penetration of the 'scientific state' as a key component of the wider processes of modernization. Essentially this means that a bureaucratic state seeks to use science and the latest technology to enhance its effectiveness and efficiency in both internal and external affairs. If the state's economic control is now being challenged by the vast transnational companies and practices that dominate much of the globe, if its military preponderance has been limited first by the superpowers' nuclear dominance and then by the internationalization of command structures and military technology, its social and cultural power and penetration have, if anything, been enhanced, despite the unprecedented transformations resulting from computerized information technology and global mass-communications systems.

This may be briefly illustrated in three areas: public education, the mass media and cultural and social policy. All three bear closely on the ethnic character and national identity of the state's population.

Public education is deemed by some theorists to be central to the production of a 'high', literate culture and hence homogenous nation. Certainly, most governments since the end of the nineteenth century have seen it as one of their prime duties to establish, fund and increasingly direct a mass system of public education – compulsory, standardized, hierarchical, academy-supervised and diploma-conferring – in order to create an efficient labour force and loyal, homogenous citizenry. This was the explicit aim of the French Third Republic after France's defeat in the Franco-Prussian War in 1870. A mass, standardized, public education system was established as one of the key instruments for unifying and creating 'Frenchmen', able to resist Prussia and reconquer the territories of Alsace and Lorraine lost after the French defeat in that war. To this end, new practices of physical fitness and new ideals of Greek athletic beauty were adopted, displacing the earlier intellectualist and Catholic disdain of the body and physical activity. The leaders of the Republic also used the teaching of a standard history through the common Lavisse textbook at various school grades to inculcate a shared sense of France's past greatness, of its heroes and virtues, and its pre-eminent place among the nations. The criterion of greatness was largely territorial: the ability to expand France's borders and integrate and unify its inhabitants. Thus Richelieu and Louis XIV scored high, despite their monarchical aims, while the account of Napoleon, for all his original republican patriotism, was deeply ambivalent: he had, after all, by 1814–15 lost most of the territories France had gained in the Revolutionary Wars. Even more important, the delineation of French grandeur going back to Clovis was based on the dynastic succession and the persistence of the territorial hexagon at the core of the concept of the French realm and state. And it was this nationalist history that French (and colonial) children had to learn in every school at every grade by state decree.[8]

Equally important was the contemporary use of mass public education in Japan. Here, a few years after the Meiji Restoration of the Emperor in 1868, the reforming aristocratic leaders of Japan issued the Imperial Rescript on Education (1890) which laid down that loyalty to the Emperor was to be the guiding principle of mass education by the state in Japan. The aim, of course, was to emulate and compete with modern Western states and societies on their own terms, the Japanese reformers being convinced that in secular education lay the key to Western military and economic success; and to achieve this goal they instituted a large-scale hierarchical system of education to inculcate modern skills and imperial Japanese values. More recent examples of homogenization through mass, public education can be found in the new states of Africa and Asia. In most cases, standard literary and historical texts recount the contributions and history of the nation and its heroes. In other cases, notably some Islamic states, a religious dimension is invoked to support and reinterpret what are essentially nationalist aims and values. In Egypt under Nasser, for example, the Islamic Arab elements were harmonized by state education policies, despite the fact that, as in Syria, Egyptian nationalism was essentially secular in orientation. What is important is that the mass education system which inculcates these common values and outlooks is a state system under state control. In Nigeria and Kenya, in Syria and Iraq, in Israel and Egypt, in Malaysia and Singapore, the state has intervened directly to guide as well as establish and fund the mass education system.[9]

The mass media have also played an increasingly vital role in underpinning the power of the state and enabling it to penetrate the social consciousness. This was taken for granted by one-party communist and fascist states in the 1930s. In the 1950s in the Middle East, Daniel Lerner and his associates found the state's use of radio and television was making a strong impact on the middle classes. Fear of the uses of the mass media in the hands of rival organizations such as the Muslim Brotherhood drove many Arab states, even where they were not already so inclined, to take over control of the mass media, especially the radio and television stations. In the hands of (among others) the Libyan, Algerian and Iranian regimes, the mass media have expanded the role of the state and wedded it to the identity and destiny of the nation. So important have these instruments of mass communication seemed, that the first step of any coup leader has been to seize the transmitters and stations to broadcast the message of liberation, and the state in turn has realized the vital importance of retaining them under its control.[10]

Even in the West, with its greater press freedoms and more liberal traditions of state intervention, there is a high degree of state regulation of radio and to a lesser extent of television. Even where there is greater freedom, the content of many transmissions, whether of news or documentaries or even drama, is distinctly national in flavour and bias: the world is still largely seen through the lens of one's national state.

The state's intervention in and control over cultural and social policies has also markedly increased. The emergence of 'official' cultural nationalism in European states in the later nineteenth century is a familiar story, with policies of Magyarization, Russification and Germanization (of Poles in the Poznań area). By the twentieth century the state's cultural nationalist policies had become more sophisticated. In Mexico from the 1920s, the post-revolutionary regimes of Obreron and Vasconcelos framed an all-embracing policy of cultural nationalism based on the idea of a 'fusion of the races' and a union of their very different cultural heritages under the aegis of the Mexican state. Making use of the archaeological discoveries of Teotihuacan, the researches of such anthropologists as Manuel Gamio and the talents of such painters as David Alfaro Siqueiros, José Clemente

Orozco and Diego Rivera, the state commissioned and pre-sented to the people a panorama of successive cultures through which a modern myth of the fusion of races, *mestizaje*, could be traced back to the pre-Colombian past, and in this way the lineage of the modern national state could be firmly rooted in a millennial Mexican past. At the same time, the modern national state could be presented as the legitimate heir and synthesis of the different successive cultures – Indian and Hispanic – that composed the culture area and heritage of Mexico, at the expense, one should add, of the indigenous 'Indian peoples'.[11]

In the twentieth century, too, the cinema has been a potent means for presenting state cultural policies and national ideals that can reach millions. Sergei Eisenstein's great his-torical films such as *Potemkin*, *Alexander Nevsky* and *Ivan the Terrible* were able to crystallize and disseminate the sense of the Russian nation and (Soviet) state under threat from enemies within as well as without, to millions of Soviet citizens. Other great directors – Akira Kurosawa, Luis Buñuel, Ingmar Bergman, Satjayit Ray, Andrej Wajda – were also able to convey a sense of national individuality by re-creating through the camera unique national landscapes, legends and atmospheres, past and present. Most of them operated outside specific state policies, or were critical of them, but their works conveyed a sense of separate national history and destiny, indirectly underlining the attachments of citizens to their national states. In our day, too, the symbiosis of state and nation has been intensified through growing ministerial control over all aspects of cultural and social policy. This is patently clear in the field of education, and especially higher education, but it has become increasingly manifest in many other areas like regulation of the press, radio and television, medicine and health services, the liberal professions, labour law, family status and benefits, genetic engineering, criminal justice, policing and prison services. Through the use of the latest advances in science and technology, the bureaucratic state has been able to penetrate every area of professional and social life, extending its spatial range into the remotest corners of its territorial domain and to every household in each region of the country.[12]

Yet this very power and penetration has produced a deep crisis of legitimacy and cohesion in the modern national state. As discussed above, few states are mono-ethnic and so genuine nation-states. Most are plural 'national states', and many of them possess large ethnic and regional minorities. These minorities are of two kinds: scattered immigrant minorities, often from former colonial possessions overseas, and resident territorially compact minorities, often of long standing. The former usually live and work in a climate of discrimination, marginalization and racism, whereas the latter are today generally viewed as 'legitimate', if less favoured, co-residents of the national state, who had in earlier periods experienced neglect and discrimination on the part of elites of the dominant *ethnie*. Now, both kinds of ethnic minority increasingly represent a fracturing of the homogeneity and purity of a national identity that was pictured as an organic whole for didactic and political purposes. In this familiar 'pedagogical narrative', immigrants, ex-colonials and the marginalized – and it may be added, the co-resident 'peripheral' *ethnies* – are increasingly felt to undermine the fabric of the nation by their demands for separate but equal treatment, their cultural differences and their aspirations for diversity and autonomy. And these perceptions are grounded in a social transformation wrought by the very expansion and penetration of the national state itself, and by its project of national acculturation and homogenization.[13]

The spread of national public education, of the national mass media and of national bureaucratic cultural policies to the minority *ethnies* and the peripheries, and the state's attempts to acculturate, even assimilate, immigrants, ex-colonials and marginals, into the culture of the dominant *ethnie*, have met with only partial success. The national state has managed to establish a national system of education and compel most minorities and immigrants to put their children through its uniform schooling system, or variants of it. It has also managed to bring minorities and immigrants within the compass of the electronic media, while its cultural policies – in the arts and museology, in universities and colleges, in the regulation of the press, radio and television, in the uses of science and medicine, in family values and so on – have embraced most areas of work and leisure of immigrants and minorities. On the other hand, state penetration and modernization have too often been accompanied by a failure to deliver on its economic and social promises: of full employment, better housing, more educational resources, better health care and so on. These failures have, of course, been general. They have affected the whole population, but they bear most heavily on the poorer, the less educated and the more peripheral sectors of the national state. By its actions and failures, the over-extended state has helped to galvanize protest and provoke resistance to its insistent pressures for regimentation and its consequent discrimination against the poorer and less well-educated ethnic and regional minorities. The very instruments of communication, mobilization and participation which it used to incorporate and assimilate its citizenry have been turned against the national state and are used to question and even deny the national basis of its power and legitimacy.

Here two kinds of critique of the state's power and legitimacy, and two types of current crisis in which the state finds itself, must be distinguished. The first is external, the crisis – and critique – of its military and economic power in a world of giant transnational companies, military blocs and continental associations linked together by electronic mass communications. The second crisis and critique is internal, a challenge both to the efficacy of the national state and its legitimacy and representativeness as a national state answering to the needs and interests of its citizens. It is this latter challenge that I want to examine, through an exploration of the problems of two kinds of national identity and types of national political order.

Problems of civic and ethnic nationalisms

The theory of the national state has generally assumed a civic form of nationalism. The ideal of the sovereignty of the people has always presupposed a clear vision of the nature and boundaries of the 'people' who constitute the citizens of the national state. It is through membership of a 'people' that individuals are accorded the rights and duties of citizenship. Only members of a people can be citizens and receive the benefits of modernity which only citizenship of a national state can confer. Only those who share in the public culture of the people, who adhere to the 'civil religion' of the national state, are entitled to a share in those rights and duties which constitute citizenship. If the rights and duties of the individual citizen are in principle universal, and presuppose a uniform basis applicable across the globe, they are in practice open only to individuals who are, or have become, members of a people. Thus the Jews, emancipated by the French Revolution, had to divest themselves of their ethno-religious particularity in order to become 'universal' individuals 'like everyone else' and receive the benefits of modernity by becoming citizens. But in practice they exchanged one ancient collective particularity for another, more modern one. To receive the benefits of modernity, they had to become citizens of the national state of France, and embrace a French public culture, including the French language and French history and schooling.[14]

In France as in Wilhelmine and Weimar Germany, the Jews tried hard to assimilate, but in the end succeeded, if at all, only in individual cases. The forces of anti-Semitism – economic, social, racial, but grounded in earlier, mainly religious, definitions and antagonisms – did not permit any large-scale, collective assimilation. This is not simply another example of the general 'survival' into the modern era of pre-modern categorizations and hatreds. It also springs from the internal contradiction at the heart of the national state between a universal conception of citizenship, with its uniform rights and duties, and an inevitably particularist conception of the 'people', i.e. the community of which each citizen is a member. Here we have to return to the ethnic basis of so many nations. The communities themselves are often descended from pre-modern peoples and have inherited their memories and traditions, symbols and myths and values: 'the people' are the heirs of these 'peoples' and usually retain some of their ethnic ties and characteristics. Though the national state may be 'born anew', in Year One of the Revolution, its members and the community they form possess antecedents, a pre-history of subordination, wandering, exile, suffering, but a pre-history nonetheless and hence a sense of shared experience that marks that people off from others and endows it with a feeling of belonging.[15]

But it is not simply a question of ethnic lineage. Very often there is a strong shared conviction of moral superiority, a sense of the centrality and irreplaceability of the culture values of the national community, which can be traced back to the earlier cultivation of a myth of ethnic election by elites of pre-modern *ethnies*. Whereas in the past such myths were fundamentally religious in character, today they are often secularized expressions of ethnic superiority, at least in their official versions. Even today, beneath the public version there is often a deeper religious content to the sense of value and dignity of the national community, one which inevitably lends an air of exclusiveness to the core ethnic community of the nation. This is a sense of national dignity and chosenness that exists in France as much as in South Africa, in the United States as much as in Israel or Japan, in Australia as much as in Sri Lanka.[16]

In other words, modern nations are simultaneously and necessarily civic and ethnic. In relation to the national state, the individual is a citizen with civic rights and duties, and receives the benefits of modernity through the medium of an impersonal, and impartial, bureaucracy. Hence the nationalism of the national state is bureaucratic as well as civic. For the national state is institutionalized, and represented, through the bureaucracy and its organs in their relations with its citizens. So the bureaucracy and its staff increasingly forms the locus of the nationalism of the national state, not simply in terms of the material and status interests of the incumbents of bureaucratic offices, but in terms of the power and unity and interests of the national state itself whose representatives, both internally and externally, are the civil servants and functionaries who work for the organs of the national state and execute its laws and policies.

However, in relation to the ethnic community or 'the people', individuals are members with ties and affinities based on history and vernacular culture and for that reason are accorded the rights of citizenship (and the benefits of modernity) of the national state that represents, contains and protects the community. Hence the nationalism of the national community, of the territorial community of history and culture, is popular as well as ethnic. For the nation and its identity is expressed and revealed in the 'authentic' memories, symbols, myths, heritage and vernacular culture of the 'people' who form a community of history and destiny, and whose intellectuals and professionals seek to authenticate, safeguard and embody that heritage and culture through cultural and educational institutions in an autonomous homeland. The need for protection, recognition and belonging encourages the nation and its members, especially its intellectuals and professionals, to seek to institutionalize their symbols, culture and heritage in and through a national state which will both embody that heritage, symbols and culture and fulfil these needs. So the intellectuals and professionals who guard and run the cultural and educational institutions in the autonomous homeland or national state form the locus of the nationalism of the popular ethnic nation; they do so not just in terms of their material and status interests, but as an expression and embodiment of the identity, unity and autonomy of the people of the nation, who are generally represented by ethnic intellectuals and professionals who direct the nation's cultural policies and authenticate its heritage, culture and symbols on behalf of 'the people'.[17]

The nation, on this reading, represents a sometimes uneasy but necessary symbiosis of ethnic and civic elements, built up on bureaucratic and popular-professional social bases. The success of any nation in the modern world is dependent on this symbiosis and these social bases. This alignment of social forces, the one able to command the organs of state, the other to mobilize the energies of the people, is mirrored in the convergence of civic and ethnic elements, in which the people are seen as simultaneously citizens and ethnic members. When this symbiosis is almost perfect, when there is no fissure between the civic and ethnic components, culture and citizenship reinforce each other and the capacities of the nation are fully realized. Conversely, when this symbiosis is undermined or rent asunder, as occurred in late nineteenth-century France during the Dreyfus Affair, when the civic or the ethnic elements come to predominate, the unity and power of the nation are impaired, and citizenship and ethnicity may be brought into conflict.[18]

It is often assumed that the intrusion of ethnic elements and sentiments of collective belonging into the life of the nation inevitably breeds exclusiveness and intolerance, and that ethnic closure is the chief basis of many of the current national conflicts that afflict the world. The common vilification of nationalism is really a condemnation of one of its most common forms, ethnic nationalism and its ethnic exclusiveness. Such a view is a gross simplification of an often complex set of issues. Ethnic nationalisms are of varying kinds and degrees, some of them relatively peaceful like the Catalan and Czech movements, others aggressive and exclusive of the kind witnessed in pre-war Germany and Italy or present-day former Yugoslavia. Besides, there is no one-to-one relationship between ethnic nationalism and exclusiveness; again, the Czech and Catalan movements stand as counter-examples.[19]

But, most important, the common view fails to grasp the nature of civic nationalism. From the standpoint of affected minorities, this kind of nationalism is neither as tolerant nor as unbiased as its self-image suggests. In fact, it can be every bit as severe and uncompromising as ethnic nationalisms. For civic nationalisms often demand, as the price for receiving citizenship and its benefits, the surrender of ethnic community and individuality, the privatization of ethnic religion and the marginalization of the ethnic culture and heritage of minorities within the borders of the national state. That was how Black elites and Jews were treated by French civic nationalism: their cultures and heritages were depreciated, their traditional religions were despised and privatized or suppressed, and their ethnicity stripped away from them. To become citizens of France, they were compelled to become black or Jewish Frenchmen.[20]

Hence, not only ethnic but also civic nationalisms may demand the eradication of minority cultures and communities qua communities, on the common assumption, shared by Marxists and liberals, not just of equality through uniformity, but that 'high cultures' and 'great nations' are necessarily of greater value than 'low' cultures and small nations or *ethnies*. So the pedagogical narrative of Western democracies turns out to be every bit as demanding and rigorous – and in practice ethnically one-sided – as are those of non-Western authoritarian state-nations, since it assumes the assimilation of ethnic minorities within the borders of the national state through acculturation to a hegemonic majority ethnic culture. The civic equality of co-nationals destroys all associations and bodies that stand between the citizen and the state, and the ideology of civic nationalism relegates the customary and vernacular to the margins of society, to the family and folklore. In doing so, it also delegitimizes and devalues the ethnic cultures of resident minorities and immigrants alike, and does so consciously and deliberately.

This deliberate and open denigration of cultures and mores other than those of the hegemonic 'civic majority' has helped to create the present internal crisis of the national state. It is not simply that the 'scientific state' has invaded every sector of society, extending its laws, regulations and demands to every class and region within its domain, without regard for ethnic and cultural differences, while failing to fulfil the economic and social expectations of the poor and the minorities – so raising the consciousness and the participation of previously silent strata and exploited regions. What has brought the issue of the 'nation-state' to a head has been its predominantly plural ethnic character, the arousal of previously dormant and submerged minority *ethnies* by the social penetration and cultural regimentation of the 'scientific state' run by elites from the dominant *ethnie*, coupled with unfulfilled popular expectations, and the resulting growing pressure of discontented minorities on the political arena of the centre and its dominant ethnic community.[21]

Reinforcing and redefining the national state

The fact that this crisis of legitimacy has affected the oldest, most firmly established, democratic national states such as France, Britain, Belgium and even Switzerland has led many people to regard the nation-state as an obsolete form of political association and to announce the end of the 'epoch of the nation-state'. Apart from external pressures of globalization and Europeanization, the evidence for this view comes from the current revival of *ethnies* below the level of the national state resulting from state penetration and ethnic majoritarian democracy. This revival, which is summed up in the slogan of 'L'Europe des ethnies', appears to threaten the integrity and question the legitimacy of the national state. We have seen the force and scope of this resurgence of ethnic nationalism in Eastern Europe and the former Soviet Union, as well as in Asia and Africa, and its ability to reshape the map of the world, despite tenacious resistance by the community of states and by individual states. Regional inequalities, the uneven distribution of cultural resources, the revival of older ethnic antagonisms, may all contribute to this resurgence, but the fundamental needs of the national state and the rapid extension of state power, not least in the colonial and post-colonial state, coupled with majority ethnic hegemony, gives to these differences, inequalities and tensions a new salience and power by first incorporating and then mobilizing excluded strata, regions and *ethnies* under the banner of an ethnic nationalism.[22]

But this kind of national mobilization does not simply dissolve old empires and national states, it creates more new national states, each based on a dominant *ethnie.* This means that the idea, numbers and structures of the national state have been reinforced by a new wave of cultural and political pluralism. Not only has the number of national states multiplied, the concept of the national state itself has actually become more firmly entrenched as the norm of political association in the modern world, and its structures have been strengthened by the trend to greater cultural homogeneity that successful ethnic secession entails. Of course, practically every secession creates further ethnic enclaves, new 'trapped' minorities. But the newly created national states are in general more cohesive and solidary, because they are organized more firmly and clearly around a dominant *ethnie* – around the Czechs, Slovaks, Slovenes, Russians, Lithuanians, Armenians or Georgians. That, at any rate, has been the aspiration of the seceders, though sometimes geography, history and demography combine to thwart these hopes, as they are doing in Bosnia, or in Latvia and Kazakhstan, where the numbers of Russians have posed new problems of cohesion and identity for these newly created republics.[23]

In generalizing about the survival or obsolescence of the national state, we need to bear in mind the following considerations:

1 As of now, the national state remains the only internationally recognized structure of political association. Today, only duly constituted 'national states' are admitted to the United Nations and other international bodies, though aspirant ethnic nations may be admitted as observers.

2 Since 1991 at least eighteen new national states have been recognized as 'successor states' and the principle of ethnic secession by popular will has been conceded, even if reluctantly. This follows a long period of general refusal upheld by the superpowers during the forty years of Cold War, and broken only in the special cases of Singapore and Bangladesh.

3 Historically, the creation of new national states has proceeded in such 'waves', usually following periods of war and treaties – after 1783, 1830, 1878, 1918 and 1945 being the most obvious cases. In other words, their creation and recognition have never been smooth nor universally accepted; they have emerged from situations of constraint and conflict which international events have suddenly transformed. We should, therefore, be careful not to pronounce too categorically on an issue that, by its nature, appears to be so explosive and unpredictable.[24]

4 Sociologically, the range of existing national states is considerable. At one end stand national states more or less completely dominated by a core *ethnie* – in Poland, Denmark and Japan – while at the other pole are those

ethnically deeply divided national states like Belgium, Canada, Lebanon, Nigeria, Zaire, Angola, India and Pakistan. In between come those many national states with a dominant or core *ethnie*, but with one or more important ethnic or national minorities like China, Vietnam, Indonesia, Burma, Iran, Egypt, Zimbabwe, Algeria, Mexico, Peru, Spain, France, Britain, Romania, Bulgaria and Georgia.[25]

5 Politically, too, there is considerable variation. Some national states are democratic, others authoritarian and unlikely to concede easily to demands from their ethnic minorities. In some national states such as post-Franco Spain and Canada, successive governments have worked hard to accommodate the ethno-national grievances of their constituent *ethnies*, while in others like the Sudan and Burma, there has been little or no concession to ethnic minority aspirations and demands. In all these cases, however, the national state remains the sole arena for the resolution of ethnic problems.

From these considerations it would appear then that, despite the wide range of social and political differences, the pre-eminence of the national state as a general norm has not been seriously challenged. What is increasingly questioned is the behaviour and effectiveness of individual states and their regimes, and the distribution of powers and resources between the constituent *ethnies* of a national state. In fact, only where there has been a failure to resolve these issues and where, often for quite different reasons, the power of the state has been shaken, and where a powerful regional or superpower patron has taken up the secessionist cause, have ethnic movements mounted a successful challenge to the existing national state and established new national states based on the seceding *ethnies*.[26]

The result has been to redefine and strengthen the concept and shape of the national state through a global process of cultural and political pluralism. This means that national-ism's ideal of a world of incommensurable but equal national states, each possessing its own irreplaceable character and destiny, already proclaimed in the nineteenth century by Fichte, Mazzini and Michelet, has come to embrace every part of the globe and has taken deep root in every continent. The older political pluralism of a Europe of sovereign states and their colonial dependencies has been transformed, re-inforced and multiplied by the nationalist principle of cul-tural pluralism, of each historic culture-community with its peculiar traditions, myths and memories, obtaining its own historic territory and, preferably, its own sovereign state. In the process, the earlier ideal of ethno-national homogeneity and purity, which even then was often breached, has been increasingly abandoned in favour of a 'dominant *ethnie*' model of civic nationalism, one that entails both a more conscious attempt to embrace the civic ideal and simul-taneously insists on the national state being underpinned by the culture and traditions of its dominant or core *ethnie*, to which most members feel they belong. This uneasy com-promise, which was characteristic of the earliest Western national states, haunts the current successor states of Eastern Europe and the former Soviet Union, where a common fear, fuelled by waves of immigrants, is that an unrestrained ethnic nationalism of the kind occurring in the former Yugoslavia, may once again succeed in plunging the region into turmoil and in redrawing the map of large areas of the world. The result, once again, is not the supersession of the national state ideal and structure, but on the contrary its proliferation and ethnic reinforcement.[27]

In the West, however, both the ethnic and the civic models of the nation have been increasingly questioned and appar-ently undermined. Again, massive immigration, the influx of ex-colonial peoples, the flood of refugees and asylum-seekers, and the impact of *Gastarbeiter*, have been the catalysts and provided the material for national redefinition and a new understanding of collective attachments and belonging. As a consequence, there have been attempts to marry the civic ideal to the more recent concept of the 'plural' nation. In this concept, the constituent *ethnies* that make up the national state are seen as the sites of emotional attachment and belonging. They are therefore given wide powers over their social and cultural life and encouraged to preserve their cultural heritages, whether through federal or customary arrangements; but the identity of the nation as a whole is expressed through the national state, its laws, public culture and foundation myths. The United States of America has provided a model for the plural concept of the nation. The historic dominance of its white Puritan Anglo-Saxon culture and language, coupled with its messianic myths of origin and foundation, have provided a firm ethnic base for its subsequent experiment in cultural pluralism. Through the English language and culture, and the legal codes and constitutional structures of its federal arrangements, the United States has succeeded in welding together successive waves and generations of immigrants since the end of the nineteenth century. This has allowed the several ethnic communities that make up the United States to achieve considerable freedoms and resources in large areas of social life, culture and even political organization – though it was long assumed that their different and alien ethnic cultures would be eroded as they adopted the American creed with its providentialist myths, ethnic heritage and public culture of the Anglo-Saxon founders. Only recently has the ideal of genuine ethnic diversity within an overall national unity based on the national state and its Anglo-Saxon public culture become more widely, though by no means universally, accepted.

The remarkable quality of American nationalism is its comprehensive fervour. The United States is one of the very few national states that has avoided a 'nationalities problem', despite its extraordinary diversity, while at the same time many groups feel a profound sense of overarching American destiny. Of course, the United States is beset by troubling racial and ethnic problems; but, because immigrants were dispersed across the continent and secured no territorial base, ethnic rivalries have not led to ethnic nationalisms (apart from a brief episode among some black groups in the 1960s). At the same time, most immigrant ethnic groups, as well as the majority of the black and American Indian populations, have subscribed to the American ideal based historically on Anglo-Saxon culture; where they have not, as with the recent wave of Hispanic immigrants, this has produced a strong, if uneven, reaction among English-speaking Americans in defence of the English language in various states.[28]

In Canada similar federal arrangements, but without the concomitant unifying myths of origin and foundation, have ensured that within an overarching national legal and political framework, the ethnic communities enjoy wide powers in the economic, political and cultural spheres. Recently, after Quebec's silent revolution, there has been a growing commitment to multiculturalism and the ideal of a plural, polyethnic nation, so much so that, together with the effects of Quebecois secessionist tendencies, the very fabric of any historic identity sustaining the Canadian federation has, many would claim, been jeopardized. In the Canadian case, the dual cultural origins of state and society, and its liberal immigration policies, have created a unique situation at the very limit of sustainable national identity.

The importance of the 'plural' model should not be exaggerated. Compared with the civic and ethnic models, it has only recently come to command support and only in a few national states, notably immigrant societies like Canada, the United States, Australia, New Zealand and Argentina. Nor has the model been without its problems. In most of these cases, there was a dominant ethnic elite – creole or Anglo-Saxon pioneers and settlers – and it was they who created the legal, linguistic and educational framework of the new national state and supplied most of its heroes and myths of origin, even if some of them have recently come under critical scrutiny. Only after some decades did large influxes of immigrants begin to change the character of the national community and pluralize its former ethno-national identity. Yet the original ethnic underpinnings have set limits on what can be admitted to the 'plural nation' without wholly undermining the community and its national solidarity. Where such limits have been unduly strained, as in Canada with its dual ethnic heritage, alternative foundation myths and a militant Francophone movement, the unity and integrity of the national state itself, and of its plural, multicultural nationalism, have been jeopardized. The central difficulty of the 'plural nation' model is revealed in its inability to secure sufficient political cohesion after abandoning both ethnic solidarity and civic uniformity.[29]

In Western Europe, too, the 'fraying at the edges', found in the received national identities of the older Western national democracies, has also operated within clear limits. The influx of large numbers of immigrants, *Gastarbeiter*, refugees, ex-colonials and aliens, has certainly altered the present character of French, British or Dutch 'national identities'. They can no longer be described in the simple, relatively homogeneous terms characteristic of the pre-war period. There are today several more 'faces' of national identity in France, Britain and the Netherlands – there had always been important variations – with new differences in colour, religion, language and the like. Yet, the historical, numerical and sociological preponderance of the long-established, hegemonic 'core' communities has largely determined the boundaries and much of the character of the changing identities of these national states – in the mores of their public life, the nature of their legal codes and institutional norms, their languages of education and politics, the content of much of the history and literature taught in their schools, and in the traditions of their culture and political life.

In all these areas, aliens, refugees, ex-colonial and immigrant communities have made vital contributions whose cumulative effect has been to modify the received character of older national identities and give them a greater fluidity and diversity of expression. But though these changes in national identity have compelled national states to redefine some of their roles and functions, they have not led to a diminution of their scope and powers. The crises of legitimacy that have accompanied these changes have in the end served to strengthen the conflation of national identity with the national state within these old-established states, if not for most of the immigrants, then at least for the core and peripheral communities. In some cases, the multiculturalism implied in attempts to accommodate some of the larger immigrant communities has produced an ethno-national backlash which proclaims the 'original character' of the dominant *ethnie* and the native traditions of the national state. Even in national states which have embraced a civic model of the nation, the ethnic nationalism of the core population is an underlying resource that can still be effectively mobilized; it can spill over into the kind of exclusive and aggressive chauvinism and racism recently seen in Europe which so many people assume to be the 'natural' expression of any and every ethnic nationalism.[30]

Once again, the changes in the character of national identities even in the established democracies of the West should not be overstated. The changes in question are all being played out in the arena of the national state, despite appeals to 'Europe' and 'the world community' and frequent use of national comparisons. Such comparisons only serve to underpin the power and centrality of the national state at the expense of stateless nations and immigrant communities.

There is as yet little evidence in many of these Western cases for a real and genuine erosion of popular national identities focused on the national state in favour of regional or immigrant ethnic communities, and for any major movement in the direction of a multicultural and 'plural' conception of the nation.

To a large extent, this is the result of the historic primacy of all-embracing ethnic and civic models of the nation, first in Europe and then outside. It is also a consequence of the nationalist drive to attach national identity to a territorial political community. This holds for both types of national identity. In the ethnic model, where the nation is conceived of as a popular community of descent and vernacular culture seeking political autonomy in its historic homeland, the nationalist drive is to mobilize the people and fuse the popular ethnic community with a territorial political community. In the civic model, where the nation is regarded as a territorialized community of citizens bound by common laws and a shared public culture and civil religion, the nationalist drive is to unify the citizen community in its national territory around a set of shared symbols, myths and memories and fuse it with an identifiable culture community. Either way, the result is to reinforce and strengthen the ideal and structures of the national state and its conflation with a popular national identity. This attempt to bring together and fuse national identity and the national state has been a leitmotif of European, and world, history, even when particular attempts at secession have failed, and cultural nationalism with limited autonomy has remained the only viable option. The principle of national self-determination, enshrined in Mazzini's Young Europe movement and, a century later, in the Charter of the United Nations (albeit with limited application), succinctly expresses the close relationship between ethnic and civic nationalisms and the drive to fuse the popular national community and identity with a territorial political identity and its national state.[31]

Conclusion

For many scholars, nationalism is a movement that seeks to equate the nation with the state. They claim that without this close linkage between nation and state, nationalism would have had little social or political significance. What has been of central importance in modern history has been not so much nationalism as such, but the phenomenon of the national state which nationalists through the principle of national self-determination have so consistently elevated and pursued. Without that linkage to the state, nationalism would have been of merely folkloric interest.[32]

There is some truth in this assertion, but it needs to be strictly qualified. The political programme of nationalism has generally involved the conquest of the state by the nation, and the fusing of a popular-national with a territorial-political identity and community, in accordance with the principle of national self-determination. This follows from some of the central tenets of nationalist ideology. The main propositions of nationalism include the idea that the world is divided into distinctive nations and that the nation is the source of all political power, the claim that the individual's supreme loyalty is to the nation, and the belief that nations must have maximum autonomy to be authentic in a world of nations. But, just as we can see that the ideology of nationalism focuses on the nation rather than the state, so in practice we find cases where maximum autonomy falls well short of statehood, and where the national community seems content with a special or a federal political status, as with Scotland and Catalonia (to date). The two observations are closely linked. It is the nation that must be nurtured, protected and rendered effective, and any framework that will afford such protection and bestow such efficacy is regarded as appropriate. The territorial state is the most obvious and best-placed candidate for such a protective role, but it is not the only one. It follows that the drive for congruence between state and nation is a frequent and powerful, but by no means an inevitable, component of nationalism.

This means that nationalism in all its varieties must be separated out from the national state, and national identity from state sovereignty. The aim of nationalism is to make the civic or ethnic nation the mould and measure of the state, to make the state bend to, and express, the will of the nation. Nationalism, from this standpoint, adds to classic democratic formulations the ideal of the historic community of citizens sharing the same public ideological culture – or, in the ethnic version, the same ancestral culture and vernacular heritage. It is the people, defined as the (civic or ethnic) nation, whose voice must be heard and whose will must be obeyed. The national state is one which hears only the voice of the people and executes only its will. In and of itself, the state is nothing but an instrument for executing the will of the nation, and the significance of nations and nationalisms resides in their capacity to mobilize large numbers of people in every area of the globe for concerted political action, through or against the state and the state system of the day.

To grasp the significance of nationalism in the modern world, it is not enough to uncover the secular drive to forge national states. The direction of that drive must be grasped: from culture to politics, from the historic culture-community to the national state of citizens. The state that nationalism aims to create is a culturally defined and culturally suffused polity; it derives its *raison d'être* as well as its character from the historic culture of its dominant *ethnie*, or more rarely from the historic cultures of more than one *ethnie*. This is true even in those cases where many of its citizens are recent additions to the national community. Once again, within each national state, it is the cohesive power and historic primacy of ethnic communities, their symbols and myths, memories and values, which are revealed in the formation and character of the civic nation.

The national state, in its turn, draws its power and sustenance from the dominant *ethnie* around which it was formed and which it in turn helped to coalesce and crystallize. It does so by expressing and giving effect to the 'will' of the people which it helps to shape into a cohesive nation with a single public culture and education system. Even where that culture has recognized variants, as in the different official languages of Switzerland, the national identity which emerges from the interplay of dominant *ethnies* and territorial states is expressed in a single public culture and a dominant set of ethnic myths and historical memories, which are usually (though not invariably) adopted by individuals and groups that adhere later to the national state, as with the French- and Italian-speaking cantons of Switzerland or the later immigrants to the United States or Australia. Such a culture is not necessarily uniform and homogeneous; it may in fact have been woven from many ethnic and linguistic strands and it may reveal subtle regional variants. But it is sufficiently common and inclusive for all the citizens to share in it at the public level, and so to endow them with a feeling of cultural affinity with members and a sense of distinctiveness from outsiders.[33]

This mutual sustenance of state and nation has ensured the survival and resilience of the national state as a form of cultural polity, and continues to do so to this day. Even when the attainment of statehood is not strictly necessary for nationalism to realize its goals – as in cases of cultural nationalism, or those of autonomy ('home rule') – it has become the normal mode of national self-realization in the modern world. This is partly because of the physical and psychological protection it affords, as nationalists are never tired of repeating; and of the general recognition that a system of national states confers on those that conform to its principles. But it is also the result of a historical development by which the first modern and highly successful professionalized states – those of England (later Britain) and France – also became

114

the models of a cohesive national identity founded on a core or dominant *ethnie*. The relatively compact Anglo-French model of the national state remains the most influential on the international market. It is more easily adapted and imitated than the American 'plural' model, given the latter's size, scale and resources, and the peculiar checks and balances of its federal Constitution, which are so ill suited to the exigencies of the smaller, poorer and later-developing 'state-nations' in Africa and Asia. Besides, the Anglo-French model was historically prior: most of these 'state-nations' owed their existence as states as well as their boundaries to the European colonial powers, notably France and Britain, and they still look to them for the basic model of how a national society and national state should be formed and sustained.[34]

As long as this mutual sustenance continues, as long as states protect and fashion national identities while drawing for their power and solidarity on the mobilized historic culture-community at their core, so long will national states remain the prime political actors in the modern world, and so long will the peoples of our planet place their loyalty and trust in the sovereign, territorially finite, national state.

5

Supra- or Super-Nationalism?

If the national state is beset by internal crises, it is also threatened by external forces. Its role as the primary economic, political and cultural actor in the world has suddenly been thrown into doubt. Though this question was touched on in chapter 1, it needs to be confronted more thoroughly, especially in the light of recent political developments in Europe.

The national state, it would appear, remains resilient, and national identities, though periodically refashioned, are not about to wither away. In these circumstances, can we seriously entertain the idea of a world without nations or nationalism, a world where national states voluntarily surrender their powers to some continental body or planetary organization which will replace the nation and the national state as the object of loyalty and passion for most people?

The question has taken on a new urgency. The fact that in the western half of Europe the national state appears to be busy divesting itself of its powers while in the eastern half it seems equally eager to reappropriate those same powers after the long Soviet winter of political passivity has heightened the sense of paradox, as have the tragic events in Bosnia on the doorstep of the European Union.

Towards regional federation?

The question is not new. Ernest Renan, in his celebrated lecture delivered in 1882 and entitled *Qu'est-ce qu'une nation?*, prophesied that there would come a time when Europe would be united in some kind of federation, but added that this was not a political possibility in his day. Over a century later, the question recurs, both in Europe and outside.[1]

It is a caution that applies particularly to the familiar argument that, with the demise of the national state, regional-continental federation is the political form that best expresses and serves the economics of the great transnational companies and the societies of a 'post-national' era. Briefly, this view holds, first, that the national state can no longer serve the needs and interests of business and the market economy of advanced capitalism, and no longer provides the locus of military technology and sovereignty; and second, that the regional-continental federation, which is best suited to the needs of transnational capitalism and as the locus of sovereignty, is especially appropriate for those populations who share a close historical bond and cultural heritage.

The first of these claims need not detain us, since this is familiar territory and has to some extent been covered in chapter 1. Our concern here is not with transnational actors and practices *per se*, only with their impact on the nation and the national state. While it is true that many economic operations and institutions transcend the national state – and have, in fact, always done so – it is equally obvious that national economies remain the standard unit of regulation and allocation of resources. It is difficult at present to see how this might be otherwise, short of a reversion to empire, or a leap into a totally unified world system comprising all humanity as a single political and economic unit. Even in terms of economic, social and political data collection, the national state remains the primary unit of comparison and 'methodological nationalism' remains the rule.[2]

Empirically, of course, a great number of transnational firms span the globe, and their activities take little account of national frontiers. At the same time, they tend to have bases in one or other industrialized state which acts as the centre of their operations; hence they are vulnerable to the regulations and policies of that state. The resources at the disposal of most transnational companies are undoubtedly vast and in many cases are much greater than the budgets of many small or new states. They do not, however, outstrip those of the most powerful national states nor do they usually control the means of violence at the disposal of even some smaller states. There is also considerable evidence of a transnational stratum of economic actors – financiers, bankers, directors – for whom national barriers are increasingly irrelevant obstacles; yet the politicians whom the transnational elites must in the end influence and persuade remain answerable to other groups within each national state, and through the ballot box, to the general population.[3]

As for military power, the internationalization of command structures has certainly lent some force to arguments that the national state is no longer the primary locus of armed force. This may also be true of the nuclear level of armaments, though recent debates in France, and over North Korea and the Ukraine, suggest a degree of caution. However, at the conventional level at which wars are actually fought, the national state remains the core unit of military technology and violence, and the main supplier and procurer of armaments. Moreover, as long as such force is retained, the national state is existentially sovereign; it can withdraw from agreements and back up its withdrawal with the requisite force, despite severe economic costs. There have been plenty of cases in history of communities prepared to incur such costs in order to be free, even to the point of death.[4]

It is the second claim that I wish to pursue here. Even if the national state retains an important role in both the economic and military aspects of advanced industrial society, might not regional-continental associations and federations serve these needs better in the long run? True, the record to date of these associations and federations is not encouraging; certainly, they have registered little in the way of political success. The union of Syria and Egypt in the United Arab Republic was short-lived, as was the inclusion of Singapore in Malaysia, or the looser union of the three East African states, Kenya, Uganda and Tanzania. Similarly with the stillborn West African federation. In other cases, federation has been under heavy strain: in Belgium, in India and in Canada. In the former Soviet Union, a centralized version of federalism broke down, and it remains to be seen whether some type of looser confederal arrangement will hold. In the case of Yugoslavia, it is difficult to imagine anything being salvaged from the wreckage of Tito's federal party state.

Those cases where federation has stood the test of time, notably the United States, Australia and Switzerland, have depended on a certain degree of initial historical and cultural affinity among the population. They were underpinned by a core *ethnie* or, in the case of the United States, a large fragment thereof. Once again, an ethnic core forms the historical and cultural substratum for a high degree of decentralization and territorial devolution, and underpins the sense of solidarity.

But regional-continental associations and federations have wider functions and deeper bases. Here I am thinking of associations founded upon cultural affinities and embracing an ideology of 'Pan' nationalism. Pan-Arabism, Pan-Africanism, Pan-Turkism, Pan-Latin-Americanism are examples. So were late nineteenth-century Pan-Slavism and Pan-Germanism, which often shaded into Russian and German irredentism. Pan-Turkism too was used for irredentist purposes by the Young Turk regime, and helped to

119

justify massacres and 'relocation' of Armenians, through appeals to the linguistic and racial affinities of the Turkic-language communities, including the Mongols![5]

The functions of such 'Pan' nationalisms are ambivalent. On the one hand, they seem to be suggesting a supersession of existing national states in the interests of much larger super-states and super-nations. On the other hand, they underpin the national state by linking it to a wider category of 'pro-tected' states and strengthening its cultural profile and his-toric identity through opposition to culturally different neighbours and enemies. They provide another set of 'border guards', a new panoply of symbols and myths, memories and values, that set the included national states apart from others. 'We are all Africans' became in the 1960s not only a slogan of the colonized and dispossessed, but also an affirmation of difference and dignity through cultural unity.[6]

From a strictly political standpoint, 'Pan' nationalism must be judged as failures. They have had some uses as political fora and regional influences, but they hardly augur a break-through in political or economic relations, which can or will supplant individual national states, if that was ever intended. On the contrary, it can be argued that their function is to normalize, and thereby legitimize, the national state. These wider continental or regional associations depend ultimately on the goodwill and cooperation of their individual members, as could be seen in the case of Saddam Hussein's defiance of the majority in the Arab League on the eve of the Gulf War. But, given that cooperation, associations of culturally cog-nate states can exert some leverage in international fora and over public opinion, partly through the use of positive stereo-types and partly through bloc votes. Even at the more limited level of interstate economic and ecological projects, cultural affinities and 'Pan' nationalist ideologies can underpin understandings and cooperation, though national states have always cooperated on specific issues and projects which they judged to be in their individual 'national interest'. It is a mistake to imagine that the national state has ever been as sovereign and independent as it likes to portray itself.[7]

Undoubtedly the rapid growth of telecommunications and the mass media have encouraged the creation of wider regional-continental networks. What needs to be explored is the degree to which regional-continental associations based on 'Pan' nationalisms can generate overarching cultures and identities that compete with, or even replace, national state and ethnic identities. For, as I shall argue, these culturally based regional associations can and sometimes do serve wider social, cultural and philanthropic needs, and so should not be written off, even in the political realm.

The European project

All this needs to be borne in mind when considering the impact on nationalism and the national state of the growing trend to European unity. It is easy to see this relationship in black-and-white terms, as a zero sum: the greater the European unity, the less the national identity of each member national state. Undoubtedly, this perception lies behind the often fierce debates between pro- and anti-Europeans in Britain and elsewhere, though it is bound up with other debates – over democratization, social welfare and enlargement of the European Union. Casting its long shadow across the continent from east to west, the 'spectre of nationalism' refuses to be exorcized.

We can begin by reconsidering the old and well-rehearsed arguments between Europhiles and Eurosceptics. Broadly speaking, Europhiles have been arguing that we must 'create Europe' as a federal – a few would say, unitary – state, and thereby end the thousand years of internecine European strife and the wars of nationalism which have wrought such carnage in the twentieth century. They go on to bolster their case by saying that Europe will thereby be restored to its former

121

position of 'great power' on the world stage, on a par with America and Japan and perhaps Russia (formerly with the Soviet Union), and that through such unity, the peoples of Europe will enjoy unrivalled prosperity within their tariff boundaries and through the operation of a free internal market in goods and labour. Anti-Europeans counter that the main reason for European unity has been the Cold War, and the need to oppose Soviet Russian and/or American power; that the internal market will benefit some major European powers at the expense of smaller states; that the closed European union will harm the Third World economically; and that a 'European club' will become politically and culturally exclusive. They also point to the enhanced possibility of German economic and political domination of a unified Europe, and the growing trend to racial and ethnic exclusiveness which a unified Europe will be forced to implement. In short, they see European cooperation as beneficial, but European unification as detrimental to the interests and wider values of European peoples. De Gaulle's 'Europe des Patries' remains their ideal.[8]

There is a parallel debate between Euro-optimists and Euro-pessimists. This is an argument about probabilities and mechanisms. For the Euro-optimist, the climate for 'creating Europe' is propitious, and the chances are high, given the European orientations of business and the support of younger generations, provided that the two preconditions of vigorous leadership and well-designed institutions are fulfilled. The Europe of the future is a Europe of institutional networks governed by the norms of a civilized social democracy, balancing market needs with human rights under the aegis of an impartial and all-pervasive bureaucracy, the Commission, and an equally respected judicial branch, the European Court of Justice. A variant of this argument holds that a strong executive must be balanced by a powerful legislature and this means a greater measure of democratic control and accountability over Euro-bureaucracies.

The Euro-pessimists consider the chances of European unification at any but the most superficial (and bureaucratic) level to be fairly remote, and the rising tide of ethnic nationalism to postpone the European project even more. However incisive the leaderships and secure the institutions, they will not avail to forge any genuine European unity at the popular level unless and until there has been a commensurate evolution of popular perceptions, sentiments and attitudes away from the nation and the national state towards an overarching European identity. The Europe of the future, if it should ever emerge, will be one of mass identification and loyalty to the European ideal, alongside or even in place of national allegiances and identities, such that large numbers of the inhabitants of the European continent will not only consider themselves to be first and foremost 'Europeans' but will be prepared to make sacrifices for that ideal.[9]

Behind these arguments lie very different evaluations of what has served to bind individuals in Europe, namely, the nation and national identity. The economic arguments and political hopes and fears often conceal the much more elusive and baffling issue of national culture – the values, symbols, myths, memories and traditions that bind peoples together and confer on them a special significance and destiny. What is the nature of this heritage and culture for each community? How has it changed in the last few decades? And what will be the impact of 'Europe' on these cultures and identities?

There are two points to bear in mind here. The first is the different import of cultural identities at the individual and the collective levels. At the level of the individual, identities are multiple and often situational. As mentioned in chapter 2, human beings have multiple identities – of family, gender, class, region, religion, *ethnie* and nation – with one or other at different times taking precedence over the others, depending on many circumstances. At home we may feel we belong, and in fact belong, to a particular class or region; abroad we may see ourselves, and be seen, as members of a particular

123

ethnic or national group. For some purposes, religious community will define our identity, for others it will be gender or family. In practice, we tend to slide between these identities with relative ease, according to context and situation. Only occasionally do these multiple identities cause friction; and only rarely do they come into real conflict.[10]

Yet identities are not only 'situational'. They can also be 'pervasive'. At the collective level, it is not the options and feelings of individuals that matter, but the nature of the collective bond. Through socialization, communications and sometimes coercion, we find ourselves bound by particular identities from birth. We may seek to resist their power, but our efforts may prove unavailing. This is frequently the case with ethnic and national bonds. They are good examples of what Emile Durkheim would have described as the general, external and binding quality of social facts. From generation to generation, such bonds exert a powerful presence over our lives, and may remain durable and resilient forces, irrespective of the defection of even large numbers of individuals. The survival of some very ancient ethnic groups and nations despite individual defection and attrition – from the Armenians and Jews to the Chinese and Japanese – is evidence of the persistence of at least some ethnic ties and boundaries over millennia, despite periodic transformations of their cultural contents and enforced mass expulsions and defections of their members.[11]

Theoretically, then, it would be perfectly possible for the peoples of Europe to feel that they had more than one collective cultural identity: to feel themselves Sicilian, Italian and European, or Flemish, Belgian and European (as well as being female, middle class, Muslim or whatever). At the same time, it should also be asked: what is the relative strength of these 'concentric circles of allegiance'? Which of these circles is politically decisive, which has most effect on people's day-to-day lives? And which of these cultural identities and loyalties is likely to be more durable and pervasive?[12]

124

The second point to note is that European unification, if and when it comes, has meant and can mean very different things, depending on the level sought. In everyday parlance, it often means simply the creation of a common market, without any political connotations. Alternatively, it may signify a commitment to federalism, seen as the fulfilment of economic union. Neither meaning carries any reference to a cultural level of unification. There is often a tacit assumption that federalism entails some measure of cultural convergence, at least in terms of an overarching European identity and community which includes existing national identities. But this is to conflate politics with culture; though they may be closely linked in particular cases, these levels should be kept separate.[13]

The modern trend may be to seek to equate national identity with the national state, but to pool sovereignties is not the same thing as fusing cultures or amalgamating identities; and the creation of a European 'super-state' is not the same as forming a 'super-nation' of Europe. The late eighteenth-century partitions of the Polish state, for example, did not spell the end of a Polish people and a Polish culture. The conquest of the Catholic Irish tribes by the Protestant English and the Union of England and Ireland after 1800 actually strengthened a native Irish culture and a sense of common Irish ethnicity. Nor does economic and monetary union entail the loss of one's culture or heritage. After all, Walloons and Flemish, Scots and English, Basques and Castilians, are bound in economic and political unions, but none of these *ethnies* and nations have lost any of their cultural distinctiveness. We can hardly imagine, then, that a European economic and political union, or a European federation, will abolish or erode the deeply ingrained historic identities and cultures of the very diverse peoples of Europe.[14]

Whether such a political union or federation is as desirable as it is possible is another matter. That the creation in a couple of decades of some form of federative union can be envisaged for much of the European continent is not in question. How deeply it will penetrate, how far its powers will really encroach on those of its constituent national states in vital matters, is debatable. But all these probabilities should not be confused with the quite separate question of creating a common European culture and a shared European identity.

A European identity?

There are two contrasting models for the creation of collective cultural identities. The first regards identities as socially constructed artefacts, which can be brought into being and shaped by active intervention and planning. According to this view, the creation of a European cultural identity is part of the active process of forging an institutional framework for a European political community. Just as 'Germany' as a cultural identity was created in the process of forging the Zollverein and the Bismarckian Reich, so the 'European identity' will emerge from the active will and deliberate planning of clear-sighted and strong-minded leaders and elites. In this activist and elite-centred vision, a European identity will spread in much the same way as did aristocratic ethnic culture in 'lateral' *ethnies*, that is, through a process of bureaucratic incorporation of middle and lower classes and of outlying regions by the elite-led centre.[15]

The second model views cultural identities as the precipitate of generations of shared memories and experiences. In this view, a European identity, were it to materialize, would be likely to evolve through a slow, inchoate, often unplanned process, though selected aspects might be the objects of attempts at conscious planning. As Euro-pessimists point out, economic or political unions can be deliberately created by building up common infrastructures and establishing institutions. Cultures and collective identities, on the other hand, are the product of a host of social, political and cultural traditions, values, memories and symbols at the popular level that have coalesced over time to produce a common heritage and 'mythomoteur', a constitutive political myth, in the same manner as 'vertical', demotic *ethnies*. It is only possible to envisage a truly European cultural identity at this popular level as the outcome of the shared experiences and memories, traditions and values, and unifying myths and symbols of several generations of the peoples of Europe – shared, that is, by *all* the peoples of Europe. This raises a difficult question: where shall we find such Pan-European popular traditions and values, symbols and experiences?

There are two problems here. The first is the 'top down' nature of European unification to date. The European project has been constructed functionally through the actions and programmes of business, administrative and intellectual elites whose needs could no longer be fully met within the context of the national state and who have sought to build the economic infrastructure and political framework of a wider European union. On this reasoning, mass culture lags behind elite economic and political action, and requires a period of stabilization to catch up with economic and political changes, and thereby fulfil its functions in the division of labour. Where the political elites lead, the masses will follow as a result of the 'downward filtration' of new elite ideas, practices and institutional norms.[16]

The difficulty with this functional approach is its over-reliance on elites and leaderships. This has been amply demonstrated by the popular responses to the Maastricht Treaty's provisions in Denmark, France and the United Kingdom, and by a certain coolness towards 'Europe' in the Scandinavian candidate countries. Governments may lead but their peoples do not always appear eager to follow them into the European Union. There is a calculative quality about attitudes to Europe in many quarters that suggests an absence of deep emotional or cultural bonds between the peoples of the

127

European continent, and little sense of any distinctive value-
and belief-system shared exclusively by the peoples of
Europe. Though the desire may exist among many Europeans
to cooperate and live and work together, it does not appear
to be underpinned by any clear popular idea of what 'Europe'
stands for in terms of culture, values, ideals and traditions
nor by any vivid sense of belonging to a European family of
peoples.

This may well be connected with the second problem, the
difficulty of defining the nature of a 'European bond' and its
distinctive culture. One clue in the quest for such definition
was touched on earlier, in the discussion of 'Pan' nationalisms. These large-scale cultural nationalisms have often tried,
usually unsuccessfully, to draw together separate states
and their peoples, on the basis of shared cultural criteria and
a common cultural heritage, and weld them into a single
super-national unity. Nationalist movements of this kind
included Pan-Turkism, Pan-Slavism, Pan-Africanism, Pan-
Latin-Americanism – and Pan-Europeanism, i.e. the Pan-
Europeanism of Coudenhove-Kalergi, Jean Monnet and the
European Movement founded in 1948 in The Hague, rather
than merely a step-by-step, piecemeal approach to economic
union. It is a Pan-Europeanism that starts from the top and
works down into society, that looks to leaders and elites, to
institutions and norms, to the conscious will and planning of
trained and motivated cadres who will go out and spread the
message of European unity and create the European bond as
the only realistic solution to the many ills with which the
peoples of Europe have long been afflicted.[17]

Pan-Europeanism was, and is, a grand vision, one that
places culture at the heart of the new Europe and seeks to
create by institution and ordinance a new European culture,
indeed a new European man and woman. But here lies the
problem. Why should anyone choose a 'European' culture
and identity over any other? On what basis can such an

128

appeal be made and why might we expect it to resonate, and among whom?

For Pan-Europeans, the answer is straightforward. There has always been a European culture and identity, however vague and difficult to pin down and formulate. This, after all, forms the basis of their appeal. Although they may speak of a new European culture and new Europeans, they see both as modern versions of something that existed in the past but was destroyed by the national state and its internecine wars and must now be recovered and restored. In the past, European unity was founded on a Christian culture and a Catholic identity; and one should hardly be surprised therefore at the influence of Catholics in the leadership of the European Movement. Medieval Christian culture was essentially Western European, with its main axis along the Rhine from Flanders to Switzerland and Italy, its centres of population and trade in the Hanseatic League cities and its principal political centres in France, the Holy Roman Empire and the Italy of the Popes. It was also essentially an elite culture, a Latin culture of the clergy and nobles and the *haute bourgeoisie*. This is the kind of European past, an expanding, innovative and militant Christian Europe threatened by Muslim Saracens and Turks in the East, that affords a model of unity for the secularized Europe of today.[18]

Of course, nobody is advocating a return to that idealized epoch of Christendom. It is the form, not the content, that provides the model. Modern Europe must find a secular equivalent of the common faith and value-system that bound Europeans of an earlier epoch together. But this only serves to compound the problem: where shall that common faith and value-system be found? Which memories and symbols, myths and traditions, can possess potency and evoke loyalty for the inhabitants of modern 'Europe'?

'Pan' nationalism, in the form of the Pan-European ideal, then, simply underlines the problem without providing any

new solutions. Should one look elsewhere, to the often frag-
ile, invented, hybrid and ambivalent character of many identities and cultures in the late twentieth century? The same
ambivalence, hybridity and fragility of the cultural artefact
can be found at the European, continental level as on the
national level of identity. In this sense, one might well speak
of a European 'family of cultures', in the manner of
Wittgenstein's concept of a 'language game', for there are
several partial, ambiguous and overlapping cultural and
political traditions, values and experiences that have over
the centuries cross-fertilized many areas and peoples on the
European continent. Several of these overlapping inter-
European traditions, values, symbols and experiences which
have affected the peoples of Europe in different ways and in
varying degrees, could be used to construct the 'imagined
community' of the new Europe, even if it remains largely an
elite affair. Over large areas of the European continent, the
elites of most (though not all) of its peoples have adopted
such traditions as Roman law and jurisprudence, the Judeo-
Christian system of ethical values, Renaissance humanism,
the Reformation and Counter-Reformation and the Enlightenment spirit. They and their peoples have also shared, albeit
differentially, in such social, political and cultural experiences as the great discoveries and colonialism, the great
revolutions, the dislocations of capitalism, industrialism and
urbanization, the movements and symbolism of romanticism,
realism and nationalism.

Nationalism? The division of Europe into warring nations?
What about those other shared mass experiences which owed
so much to nationalism, the two internecine European and
World Wars? Have not all these traditions, symbols and
experiences had their ambivalent, dark and divisive sides?
Even at the height of Catholic Christendom, were not minorities such as heretics, lepers and Jews, though inside
Europe, put outside European society, often in walled quarters, and did they not thereby define 'Europe' to itself through

the mirror image of the Other? Did not the Renaissance light up some parts of Europe only to leave others in darkness? Did not the truths of the Reformation and Counter-Reformation spawn the bloody massacres of the Wars of Religion? In short, common experiences and traditions, shared symbols and values, have simply highlighted Europe's overlapping diversity, sharpened its ethnic and religious divisions and ambiguities, and revealed a kaleidoscope of distinctive *ethnies* and counter-cultures, of indigestible minorities, immigrants, aliens and social outcasts.[19]

The sheer number of these minorities and the vitality of these divided *ethnies* and their unique cultures has meant that 'Europe' itself, a geographical expression of problematic utility, has looked pale and shifting beside the entrenched cultures and heritages that make up its rich mosaic. Compared with the vibrancy and tangibility of French, Scots, Catalan, Polish or Greek cultures and ethnic traditions, a 'European identity' has seemed vacuous and nondescript, a rather lifeless summation of all the peoples and cultures on the continent, adding little to what already exists; alternatively Europe has become merely an arena, a field force, for conflicting identities and cultures.[20] in comparison with the

Worse, a European identity commands little mass affection or loyalty. It is a bit like virtue. Everyone is for virtue, as Eurobarometer is always telling us; everyone, that is, except the English (and sometimes the French), who seem to be indifferent to, if not downright sceptical of, European virtue. But even committed Europeans cannot summon up that intimacy of feeling, that warmth and even love, that one's *ethnie* or nation can so often inspire. If 'nationalism is love', to quote Michel Aflaq, a passion that demands overwhelming commitment, the abstraction of 'Europe' competes on unequal terms with the tangibility and 'rootedness' of each nation. Thus painters and poets have recorded and praised the beauties of particular places in Europe, or of specific regional, ethnic or national scenes, associated with unique histories and traditions, but never the 'European landscape' in general. And the same is true of the novelists who depict the panorama of social life in specific villages, towns and countries of Europe.[21]

The abstract quality of a European identity is, of course, no accident. As we saw, to impart warmth and life to that identity would mean dredging up memories best left alone; memories of wars, of expulsions, of massacres by and of the peoples of Europe, let alone of outsiders, recent and painful memories. For Renan, forgetting was as important to the nation as remembering. Selective memory, and a quantity of amnesia, is essential for the survival of nations. But can we choose what we shall forget? How do we wipe away, if wipe we should, the recent memories of the Holocaust? And does the present allow Europeans the luxury of amnesia? The revival of anti-Semitism, neo-Nazi attacks on immigrants and *Gastarbeiter*, the re-enactment of ethnic cleansing on the soil of Bosnia, the spectre of a Balkan war over the very name of Macedonia, all have raised the question of whether the peoples of Europe are being condemned to repeat what they do not care to remember.

There is a more fundamental issue here, the role of memory in collective identity. Can any collective cultural identity come into being or sustain itself through a complete break with the past? Have not the revolutions of the past had to accommodate themselves in some measure to the pattern of values, traditions, symbols and memories of earlier generations of the society in which they erupted? Even where there was no outright restoration of an *ancien régime*, as there was in England, France and latterly in Russia, there were determined attempts to fuse different cultures in a new composite civilization of the kind pursued by Mexico's modern revolutionaries. Even the American case affords no counterexample: the Puritan fathers may have turned their backs on the mother-country, the founders of the republic may have resolved to have as little to do with the Old World as possible, but they were repeatedly drawn back into its vortex, and are repeatedly reminded of their ancestry and antecedents to this day. This suggests that for collective cultural identity shared memory is as essential to survival as is the sense of a common destiny. 'Forgetfulness leads to exile, while remembrance is the secret of redemption.'[22] By the test of memory, Europe today would fare badly.

European myths and symbols

If the European memory is haunted, if its peoples share only the painful reminders of a nationally divided past, can they perhaps unite around common myths and symbols which signal a deeper solidarity and difference? What potency and meaning can the peoples of contemporary Europe derive from such 'myth-symbol complexes' as we may find? And where shall we look for these myths and symbols?

To the Greco-Roman heritage and Roman law? Certainly, the legacy of classical antiquity is marked throughout present-day Europe – in its roads and the names of its cities, its traditions of sculpture and architecture, its laws and languages, its history and philosophy, its drama and heroic myths, its democratic and imperial traditions, its rationalism and spirit of scientific enquiry. But that legacy was then, and remains, unequally diffused over the continent of Europe. The lands of the Mediterranean were deeply imbued with classical traditions and influences, while the lands of Northern and Eastern Europe were untouched in antiquity, and felt only an after-presence from the Renaissance onwards. Moreover, they were constantly being challenged by other ideals and traditions. The vision of ancient Greece as the 'youth of Europe' may have excited some elites, particularly in the Victorian era, and left its imprint in the civilization of the modern West (including America), but it is now too remote to strike any deep chord with most of the inhabitants of Europe.[23]

Or should we look to the civilization of Christendom and its Judeo-Christian system of values? Here too the influence is deep – in the traditions of the Churches themselves and the role of the clergy, in the translation of the Bible into vernacular languages, in the wider concern with social justice and social welfare, in socialist ethics and the movements of equality for the oppressed and underprivileged, and in the many voluntary and charitable organizations. But there have also been deep divisions and ambivalent influences: the schism between Orthodoxy and Catholicism, between Catholicism and the Protestant churches, between sects and churches, affecting different areas of Europe in various ways. The myth-symbol complex of Christendom, of a Christian civilization united in the Crusades against the infidel, by its treatment of heretics and Jews within Europe and its wars on Byzantium and Muslims at its verge, through its Wars of Religion right up to its bankruptcy in Nazi Germany, has repeatedly shown itself incapable of providing that moral unity for Europe which it proclaimed and which some Europeans would now like to resurrect. The religious divisions within key areas of the European continent still run deep, even if fewer people are devout believers. Religion-as-badge, religion-as-cement, religion-as-boundary, religion-cum-ethnicity, all can be found in many of the bitter conflicts that still afflict the continent, or as an undertow to more stable, but equally deep cleavages.[24]

Perhaps we can find that symbolic and mythological unity in Europe's Indo-European heritage of language and origin? It is true that many of Europe's languages belong to the Indo-European family, and some scholars still maintain the theory of an Ur-language and an original home for the Indo-European-speaking tribes in a distant past. But archaeologists, linguists and historians are divided; there are several languages in modern Europe that do not belong to this group

134

(Basque, Finnish, Estonian, Hungarian); and, most crucially, after the uses to which the language-group-as-race theory was put by the Nazis, there is little interest among most inhabitants of Europe for the myth of an 'Indo-European heritage' outside some small, but vociferous, groups of revisionist historians, and racists.[25]

What then of Europe's white imperialist tradition and its exclusion of people of colour? Might we not find here that symbolic and mythic unity that has so far eluded us? If the Indo-European myth is a minority affair, the exclusive sense of European superiority based on colour prejudice is decidedly not. Here, certainly, is a potent and explosive set of myths and symbols that could unite 'Europeans' against 'outsiders' and create the mass emotional conditions for the policies of discrimination and exclusion practised by many governments of contemporary European states. This is undoubtedly one of the key elements in the present climate of ethnic fear and moral panic towards immigrants, asylum-seekers, refugees and aliens that some governments, some of the media and some interest groups have orchestrated in recent years in many Western European states. The question is: could such a myth of white European superiority unite Europeans and override internal differences, and can colour serve as the basis of a symbolism of Europeanness?

That it did so in the past, for some European elites at least, and that it has the power to ignite mass outbursts today, is undeniable. But that power is negative: it thrives not on shared values nor on exclusively European characteristics, but on differences that are perceived in varying ways and degrees. 'Whiteness' may end at the borders of the national state or at the edge of a village or urban district. To some, Turks are outsiders, to others Bosnian Muslims, for still others it may be Poles or Serbs or Albanians – or French or Anglo-Saxons. Two issues have given the question of the Other greater salience: immigration and Islam. The issue of immigration reinforces national, not European, identity perceptions, since it is the national state that controls immigration, the national media that diffuse information and opinions about immigrants, the national labour market that discriminates against them, and the people of the nation who are invoked when immigrants are persecuted or expelled. Hence, the sense of the non-white outsider reinforces national prejudices and national unity, albeit negatively through difference, and in no way contributes to a sense of European unity and identity.[26]

Islam, at first sight, might seem to contradict the tendency to nationalism, since it operates on a continental basis. There is certainly a widespread stereotype of Islam and Muslims that harks back to the Crusades and the long struggle with the Ottoman Turks. This Pan-European stereotype undermines the claims of Turkey, despite its official secularism and current democratic regime, to be 'European' and join the European Union. The Muslim character of much of its population and its historic enemy role make it suspect for most 'Europeans'. On the other hand, Islam also presents challenges to individual European national states and hence fuels their nationalisms. In France, the size of the Muslim community has increased support for Le Pen's movement, while the size of the Turkish and other minorities, denied citizenship in Germany, has sparked violence and racial hatred, stirred up by the neo-Nazi movement. In Britain, too, there have been disturbances occasioned by Islamic issues such as the Rushdie affair, and these in turn have raised the question of a British national identity and its relationship to Englishness.[27]

If the imperialist legacy of white, Christian exclusiveness operates mainly at the national level and reinforces national identifications, can we then find in the history of 'Europe' some measure of commonality and some heroic figures that can serve as an inspiration for a European consciousness? It is something of a vexed question whether we can speak at all of a 'European history', which is not simply a 'history of its peoples'. Within the continent of Europe, we find a variety of sequences and streams of events which affect its different areas at different times. I have already alluded to certain patterns of culture and some traditions that have variously filtered through the peoples of the continent, but we have seen that even these cannot be pressed too far. The idea that there are any large common themes which the various developments within Europe illustrate greatly overstrains the historical evidence and must be seen as part of the Pan-European mythology which is being constructed by certain interest groups and elites today. This much, at least, is clear from the semi-official history of Europe compiled by Jean-Baptiste Duroselle.[28]

Given this situation, can we yet find some great exemplars of European humanity and heroism? To whom shall we return? To Augustus who mourned the loss of Varro and his legions in the Teutoberg forest and relinquished the other half of Europe? To Charlemagne and his successors whose Holy Roman Empire was equally based in the West and whose medieval ideals have no resonance for modern secular, democratic Europeans? To Napoleon whose ambition and empire was as short-lived, and unattractive, as that of any modern dictator? Should we turn instead to the great 'European' artists, writers and scientists – to a Shakespeare, a Michelangelo, a Beethoven and an Einstein? But their genius is universal, their art and science transcends all boundaries, and as for the lesser talents, they have generally been nationalized, in the Romantic tradition, and their national influence is often greater than any European or global appeal.[29]

There is another problem with these attempts to build Europe around its history, its myths and its symbols. For the most part, the examples come from Western Europe and Italy. The exemplars of Eastern Europe, with significant exceptions such as Copernicus, Chopin, Tchaikovsky and Tolstoy, have little meaning for a predominantly Westernoriginating 'Europe', or in cases like Ivan the Terrible or Peter the Great evoke only fear or revulsion. As for the myths and symbols of Eastern Europe, compared to those of the Renaissance or the French Revolution, they are local, unfamiliar and suspect outside the lands of their origin, with the possible exception of the Greek War of Independence. Once again, the predominance of Western Europe is underscored, not just in its centres of wealth and technology, population and trade, but in its science, literature, education and arts, and in the production and dissemination of its popular myths, symbols and traditions.[30]

It would appear, then, that there are hardly any common *European* myths and symbols that can have meaning and potency for the modern inhabitants of the continent of Europe, and can serve to unify them. There are too many lacunae, too many zones of exclusion and incomprehension, like the lands of the Orthodox Churches with their very different social structures and cultural traditions, outlooks and symbolism, or the many non-Christian minorities and outsiders – from the persecuted Jews of the Middle Ages to the persecuted *Gastarbeiter* of today – who can find little in a Europe that harks back to the ideal of medieval Christendom. The most potent 'myth-symbol complexes' in the continent of Europe are much more powerfully national in origins and context than European, be they the myths and symbols of Roman *imperium* or the Enlightenment and the French Revolution, the Risorgimento or the Bolshevik Revolution.[31]

Nor can one easily find European holy centres or shrines of pilgrimage for all Europeans. Aachen is too remote, St Paul's, Les Invalides or Wawel too national, and even Rome no longer commands the hearts and minds of peoples in the north and west of Europe. In this respect, nationalism has pre-empted Pan-Europeanism. Its shrines and monuments are everywhere. They occupy the official centre – in the Arches of Triumph and the Tombs of the Unknown Soldier – and the many popular peripheries. The nation's statuary, its flags and emblems, its temples and memorials, dominate the hills, fill the squares and decorate the town halls, reminding the citizens of their allegiance and evoking their pride. Beside these memorials of stone, what has 'Europe' been able to offer? Can its emblems evoke the same passions as those of its nations?[32]

Can one perhaps speak of commensurable *European* rites and ceremonies that will fill the hearts and inspire the imaginations of all the inhabitants of the continent, in the same way that Washington, the Constitution and Independence Day can unite the hearts and inspire the imaginations of most Americans in the United States? Perhaps in time, over several generations, such rites will emerge, such ceremonies come into being, centred on the European Parliament in Strasbourg and the seat of the Commission in Brussels. The trouble, however, with all such 'invented traditions', is that their creators cannot be sure that their inventions will find a deeper response in the next generation. In this respect, nationalism is always one step ahead: it has always had its eye on the judgement of posterity, with which it seeks to replace an other-worldly salvation.[33]

Without shared memories and meanings, without common symbols and myths, without shrines and ceremonies and monuments, except the bitter reminders of recent holocausts and wars, who will feel European in the depths of their being, and who will willingly sacrifice themselves for so abstract an ideal? In short, who will die for Europe?

It is not much of an answer to point to a common security and foreign policy which will commit a 'European force' to overseas or European theatres of war, or to the popular response when the first 'European soldiers' are killed. In fact, the European record has not been encouraging to date in this respect. It was the UN led by the United States that undertook the invasion of Kuwait in 1990 and it has been NATO rather than the European Union that has taken the initiative in 1994 in Bosnia, in an ethnic conflict clearly occurring within the borders of the continent of Europe itself. The history of common European defence and foreign policy initiatives has been marked by dissension and misunderstandings, most recently over Bosnia and Macedonia. The European defence units remain small, and there is little popular support for defence integration or for military ventures, even within the heartlands of Europe, and even less at Europe's borders, variously defined as stretching from Ireland to Macedonia and the Baltic states or from France to the Caucasus and the Urals.[34]

Military sacrifices, too, are inevitably portrayed in a national rather than European context. However they are officially presented, such sacrifices are interpreted by press and people alike as those of the nation, and any real mourning will be reserved for fellow-nationals, not for 'Europeans'. The ethnic nation has always presented itself as the 'family of families', the summation and union of every family within the community. Its myth is that of the 'super-family' of shared fictive descent and common 'blood'. This means that over the generations, members of an ethnic community or nation have learnt to see and feel themselves as part of a large, extended family; so national defence is felt to be a necessary sacrifice for one's kith and kin, for one's family.[35]

Compared with this vivid and tangible, if fictional, national family, the European 'family of cultures' appears pale and skeletal. Like a shell, in which the nations, regions and *ethnies* of Europe can take shelter, the European project affords a framework for working out problems and securing benefits for the peoples of Europe, but it appears to constitute no deep bond, no living force, no community of faith. This may indeed be one of its chief attractions for all those regions and minority *ethnies* that loudly proclaim their allegiance to the new Europe; under the European umbrella, the primary loyalties of the people will return to where they belong, away from the powerful national states and back to the neglected and oppressed *ethnies*. 'L'Europe des Ethnies' expresses this goal succintly. But, on the obverse of the same coin is inscribed 'L'Europe des Patries'.[36]

A 'European super-nation'?

Neither goal fulfils the Pan-European dream. For Pan-Europeans, Europe is neither a cooperative venture between the existing national states, nor an umbrella protecting the many *ethnies* and regions which are straining at the leash of the national state. It is a genuinely 'supra-national' union, which would truly transcend the narrow outlook of the nation and obliterate the ugly face of nationalism. But would such a union in fact transcend the nation and supersede nationalism, as the Pan-Europeans so devoutly hoped? Or would we be witnessing the growth, not of some novel 'supra-national' unit, but of another old-new nation writ large, a European 'super-nation', with its own flag, anthem and capital in Brussels, its passports, coinage and bank, its parliament, defence forces and foreign policies, universities and academies, annual festivals, ceremonial parades and processions, monuments for the fallen, memorials for its founders, and its museums of European history and folklore? And would not such a super-nation merely compound the problems of a world of nations? In that case, European unification, far from sounding the death-knell of nationalism, would raise it to a new level of power and legitimacy.[37]

This is the fear, not merely of the nationalists of existing national states, but of Euro-pessimists for whom 'Europe' can only arise in the image of the nation and with the same features and gestation that gave birth to the nation. They argue that, while so large and diverse a union will have some novel features – those, in fact, of a polyethnic nation – it must, like any long-term human association, develop those

141

fundamentals of collective identification – of shared memory, myth, value and symbol – that any cultural grouping must generate if it is to survive for several generations. In the European context, the only way in which a truly united Europe could emerge is through the slow formation of common European memories, traditions, values, myths and symbols, in the image of the *ethnie* and the nation.

But, as explained above, in these respects the concept of Europe is deficient. While some cultural and political traditions are to hand, they are marked by ambivalence and uneven penetration, and there are no overarching shared memories, myths and symbols which can unite Europeans, apart from the unusable ideals of medieval Christendom or imperialism. Even more to the point, any attempt to construct a European identity around these shared cultural elements must compete with the pre-existing and deeply rooted ethno-national myths, symbols, values and memories of the nations and *ethnies* which make up the conventionally designated geographical area of Europe.

It is this ethno-symbolic competition that makes the achievement of European unity so unlikely in the foreseeable future at the cultural and social psychological levels. While some mobile elites may have broken loose from ethno-national attachments, in the tradition of medieval and early modern European aristocracies, popular attachments and mass allegiances to nations and national states remain deep-rooted and are reinforced by a variety of modern bureaucratic and cultural mechanisms, including the national education system, the national media, a national language and literature, national legal codes, as well as the more elusive yet pervasive factors of landscape, art, music, dress, food, recreations and folklore. These cultural elements are not simply populist inventions of manipulative intellectuals, nor just folkloristic vestiges of a former way of life, a romantic and nostalgic attachment to a distant idealized past – though both elements may also be present on occasion. They are components of entrenched modes of popular culture which, though they have recently undergone a more rapid pace of change, retain many of their distinctive qualities and characteristics. They are also components of a received national identity which, though also undergoing considerable modification, is still able to unite the mass of the people of that nation around a shared understanding of common values, memories, traditions and symbols.[38]

From this standpoint, the creation of larger 'supernational' entities out of sharply differentiated popular national identities must remain problematic. To transfer the loyalties and identifications of the majority of the populations of these national states and nations and attach them to a new set of shared European myths, memories, values and symbols involves a feat of cultural and social psychological engineering, in tandem with relevant institutional frameworks, that in the past was possible only with the dissolution of existing collectivities and units of association, or through mass religious movements. Since neither of these conditions seems likely to obtain in the foreseeable future and since in the meantime the national state remains resilient and there is no sign of any diminution in ethnic awareness and self-determination, there would appear to be little cultural and emotional space for a new Pan-European level of popular super-national identification to develop.

Conclusion

We can look at the European and other projects of unification in two ways: as heroic, if doomed, attempts to supersede the nation, and as new, emergent types of national community. It may be that we are witnessing another turn in the long cycle of formation and dissolution of human associations. Recorded history has always seen the oscillation of competing kinds of social and political unit, with larger units being forged out of the conquest or union of smaller units, or dissolved again into their constituent parts. The history of the great empires, followed by feudal interregna, affords the paradigm of this historical movement. Contrary to earlier beliefs, it seems unlikely that the transition to a modern, industrial type of society can break this mould, or alter the patterns of coalescence and dissolution. In this as in other respects, politics and culture have their own rhythms of change which cannot be reduced to technological and economic movements.

The difference is that in modern societies, the two movements, of coalescence and of dissolution, go hand in hand, spurred by the same forces of vernacular mass mobilization, cultural politicization and communal purification discussed earlier. This returns us to our initial paradox: the coexistence of unifying and divisive, enlarging and fragmenting trends in contemporary society and politics. I intimated at the outset that both were the product of the same general forces in modern society, and I can now spell these out more fully.

The argument I have been advancing is that attempts to create large-scale unity in Western Europe or elsewhere, whereas in most other areas of the world great multinational empires and states are dissolving into their constituent ethnic parts, result less from different levels of economic and political development than from the sheer variety of historical trajectories and the very different ethno-historical cultures of various regions and peoples. Of course, different levels of economic, technological and political development exert an important influence; but they are themselves as much the product as the producer of these diverse trajectories, ethno-histories and cultures.

In chapter 3 I described how the two most important historical routes to nation-formation in the modern world, the 'lateral' or aristocratic and the 'vertical' or demotic, greatly influenced the subsequent forms and contents of the nations that were forged out of different kinds of *ethnie*. In the one case, an elite ethnic culture was diffused outwards and downwards throughout the population by a strong and incorporating bureaucratic state, a process that was particularly prominent in Western Europe. In other parts of Europe and Asia, a popular vernacular culture of subordination and oppression remained as a living repository, an active resource, to be mobilized and politicized by native intelligentsias.

The same processes of bureaucratic incorporation by strong states and vernacular mobilization of the rural and urban masses by ethnic intelligentsias can be found in every continent, from Russia and Japan to Ethiopia, India and Mexico. The varied permutations of these historical processes help to account for the very different forms that ethnonationalism has taken in different parts of the world, and provide the basis for the insistent assertion of cultural distinctiveness and ethnic division which accompanies a growing global interdependence. Indeed, that very interdependence, by bringing disparate cultures into close proximity and revealing their differences openly, encourages ethnic and historical comparison and the proliferation of fragmenting ethnic nationalisms. When to this is added the power of modern mass telecommunications to amplify and broadcast these cultural differences and historically unique characters, our initial paradox falls into place.

Similarly, the growing interdependence of state systems in various regions of the world, as well as at the United Nations, highlights the differences of cultures and binds many people more closely to an ethno-history and heritage that they feel may be under threat. The sense of irreplaceability of one's own culture values becomes more acute when global uniformities become more salient. But it is not just a question of popular or elite reaction to perceived threats. The desire to preserve ancient values and traditions is no antiquarian nostalgia; it is the spur to a restoration of a lost community, to reliving its 'golden age', to renewing the community by purifying it of alien elements and to reappropriating its distinctive cultural heritage.

We are back with the underlying modern quest for cultural authenticity. Autonomy, the key to dignity in the modern world, requires authenticity; freedom depends on identity, and destiny on shared memory. So the desire to participate in a modern world of wide opportunities and technological expertise, requires the forging of separate moral communities with incommensurable and authentic identities. But, if the secret of identity is memory, the ethnic past must be salvaged and reappropriated, so as to renew the present and build a common future in a world of competing national communities.

It is not easy to foresee an early end to the dual process of renewal through separation and interdependence. These processes are interrelated and self-reproducing. There appears to be no easy way to break out of the circle. The very fact that ethno-histories are so unevenly diffused, that cultures are unequally politicized and that peoples are differentially mobilized in a world of mass communications and economic interdependence, suggests that, even if wider projects like European unification take root, they may well adopt some of the characteristics of existing ethnic nationalisms, spawning new and more dangerous rivalries. In these circumstances, we are unlikely to witness the early demise of national communities of history and destiny with their promise of collective immortality through the judgement of posterity.

6

In Defence of the Nation

The idea that nations and nationalisms are likely to be here for some time to come, and that this has to do with nationalism's capacity for ensuring dignity and immortality, may seem both pessimistic and perverse when we consider the excesses and outrages for which nationalists are held responsible throughout the world. Commentators are fond of attributing to nationalism many of the conflicts which infest our planet, and they tend to assume that a world without nations will be free of the attendant ills of racism, fascism and xenophobia. A world without nations, they claim, will be a more stable and peaceful, as well as a more just and free world – a dream that is in fact common to liberals and socialists for whom the nation was at best a necessary stage in the evolution of humanity and at worst a violent threat and distraction.

I want to conclude by briefly examining the arguments against nationalism and demonstrating why the nation and nationalism remain the only realistic basis for a free society of states in the modern world.

Nationalism: pro et contra

The arguments against nationalism are threefold: intellectual, ethical and geo-political.

(1) Intellectually, nationalism is held to be logically incoherent and its basic postulates untenable. These postulates are the principle of collective cultural identity, the principle of collective will and the doctrine of national boundaries.

As far as collective cultural identity is concerned, it is claimed that there are conflicting criteria for determining the national 'self'. These include language, religion, descent, customs and territory. As Max Weber showed long ago, no one of these criteria can be applied to all the collective cultural identities which claim to be or are recognized as 'nations'. In sub-Saharan Africa, for example, there is a series of overlapping 'selves', based on different criteria. Even within a single community, nationalists have espoused different criteria of the nation.[1]

The same difficulties surround the principle of the national 'will'. Apart from a daily plebiscite, there is no means of ascertaining its nature, or deciding whether it was in fact a true and free expression of the 'will of the people' or of the individuals who compose the nation. There is also the problem of deciding who shall count as 'the people'. It has been all too easy for demagogues to feel that they alone can interpret the popular will and decide who the people are.[2]

Similar problems have attended the doctrine of national boundaries. For nationalists, these are usually self-evident; they coincide, as Danton claimed for France and Mazzini for Italy, with 'natural frontiers'. But it is easy to show that such frontiers are never natural, even when they have been longstanding or distinctive; South Tyrol, for example, remains a disputed area between Italy and Austria. Inhabitants of frontier areas have a habit of refusing to acknowledge the 'naturalness' of particular borders.[3]

148

All this has led some scholars to conclude that there can be no consistent doctrine of nationalism, and that there are as many nationalisms as there are nations and nationalists.[4] This seems to be an altogether erroneous reading of the ideology of nationalism. The very fact that one can seek to analyse a set of sentiments, movements and ideas through a collective term, nationalism, suggests a certain commonality between the different expressions of these sentiments, movements and ideas. One need not deny the great variety of these expressions to concede an underlying pattern, summed up in what I have indicated (in chapter 3) is the 'core doctrine' of nationalism.

To grasp the misunderstanding in much of the critique of nationalism, it is necessary to remind ourselves of the main tenets of that doctrine and the basic ideals of nationalist movements. They are:

- The world is divided into nations, each with its own character and destiny.
- The nation is the source of all political power, and loyalty to the nation overrides all other loyalties.
- To be free, human beings must identify with a particular nation.
- To be authentic, each nation must be autonomous.
- For peace and justice to prevail in the world, nations must be free and secure.

The basic ideals that flow from these propositions are three: national identity, national unity and national autonomy. These are the goals, variously interpreted, of nationalists in every period and continent, just as the 'core doctrine' represents the *sine qua non* of nationalist beliefs, even when nationalists have added new motifs to apply the doctrine to the situation of their community. Together, the basic propositions and ideals suggest a working definition of nationalism as an 'ideological movement for the attainment and maintenance of autonomy, unity and identity on behalf of a population deemed by some of its members to constitute a "nation" '.[5]

From these propositions and ideals, there has emerged a set of symbols, myths and concepts which mark off the world of nationalism from other worlds of symbolism, mythology and discourse, and which have energized and comforted populations all over the world. Ceremonies, symbols and myths are crucial to nationalism; through them nations are formed and celebrated.

Now these propositions, ideals and definitions of nationalism and the nation make no mention of specific criteria of national identity. Any cultural element can function as a diacritical mark or badge of the nation – though it may make a considerable difference which is chosen in certain circumstances. One should not therefore castigate nationalisms for inconsistency on this score, since there is nothing in the core doctrine or ideals which lays down which cultural elements must serve as criteria of the national self. Similarly with the concepts of 'national will' and 'natural frontiers'. Nationalism does not have a theory of how the national will or the national boundaries may be ascertained; it requires other ideologies for that purpose, and so nationalism has been combined with all kinds of other movements and ideologies from liberalism to communism and racism. Nationalism's core doctrine provides no more than a basic framework for social and political order in the world, and it must be filled out by other idea-systems and by the particular circumstances of each community's situation at the time. To charge nationalism, therefore, with logical incoherence is to miss the point – and the power – of the ideological movement: nationalism combines a high degree of flexible abstraction with a unique ability to tap fundamental popular needs and aspirations, but it does not pretend to offer a comprehensive and consistent account of history and society.

(2) The ethical arguments against nationalism are, first, that it is necessarily extremist in nature; that its concern for cultural homogeneity leads to exclusiveness and social closure against minorities; and that it denies the independence, diversity and human rights of individuals.[6]

There is considerable truth in some of these arguments, especially when applied to specific instances of nationalism. But, as general arguments, they need careful qualification. The idea that all nationalists are fanatical doctrinaires of the will and that every nationalism is extremist in nature is belied by the many movements, regimes and leaders that have been on the whole democratic, liberal and moderate; the cases of Masaryk and Czechoslovakia, Prat de la Riba and Catalonia, McDiarmid and Scotland and Snellman and Finland come to mind. Outside Europe, too, we can find cases of relatively moderate nationalism, if we allow for the very different social and political circumstances: in the Ivory Coast, Zambia, Ghana after Nkrumah, Tunisia, Egypt since Nasser, Turkey since Ataturk, early Indian nationalism, Japan since 1945, Mexico since Cárdenas. Though it cannot be claimed that many regimes in the states of Latin America, Africa and Asia are democratic or liberal, their failings cannot be attributed to nationalist extremism; many other factors account for the often non-democratic nature of these regimes. The important point is that nationalism comes in many forms and degrees; they cannot be lumped together under a single rubric of 'extremism'.

Moreover, not all nationalisms have equally striven for cultural homogeneity. What all nationalists demand is a single *public* culture. There are cases where they are happy to concede some degree of private culture for ethnic and religious minorities, provided these do not impinge too much on the national identity created by the public culture of the national state. These are not, as is often thought, only cases of civic nationalisms. As mentioned earlier, civic nations can be just as severe to minorities as ethnic nations. Rather, this tolerance tends to be found in the plural nations created by immigrant societies, though it is also possible to find some toleration of minority rights in dominant *ethnie* nations like Finland, Malaysia or the former Czechoslavakia.

Nor do all nationalisms deny basic human rights and individual diversity. This is more a function of the type of secondary nationalist ideology adopted. The 'core doctrine', while demanding primary loyalty to the nation, says nothing about diversity or human rights. It is in the 'organic' version of nationalism promulgated by the German Romantics that there is a tendency to see human beings simply as specimens of their national group; but it is a mistake to regard the German Romantic doctrine as normative for nationalism, if only because French Revolutionary doctrines have been even more influential, for example in Africa, where human rights are linked to national liberation. Nevertheless, while nationalism is patently not a democratic or liberal movement, the denial of nationalism's central tenets is likely to impede progress to human rights and democracy, as Engels observed about Polish nationalism.[7]

(3) These arguments are also relevant to the main geo-political charge against nationalism: that it is destabilizing and divisive. Again, this is to overstate the case. Of course, one can point to particular cases of destabilization and division, of nationalists deliberately stirring up resentments among populations in ethnically mixed areas like Bosnia or the Caucasus. But, as the examples of the Soviet Union, Yugoslavia, Kurdistan and Ethiopia demonstrate, it is not nationalism *per se* that is responsible for the breakdown of states; nationalisms tend to emerge on the ruins of states that are, for other reasons as well as ethnic ones, no longer viable. In other cases, ethnic nationalisms may battle long and in vain, as has occurred with the Moro in the Philippines or the Nagas in India. Where states are for one reason or another no

longer viable, nationalism may offer an alternative to the often unstable (because coercive) status quo, one that is more viable because it is better attuned to popular aspirations in particular regions. The divisiveness and destabilization of so many nationalisms is simply the other side of the coin of their popular, unifying and solidaristic dimensions. Nationalism cannot be held responsible for the rivalry of states, which long pre-dated the emergence of the doctrine. What nationalism has done is to ground the competition of sovereign states on a mass cultural base, thereby providing some social cohesion in periods of rapid social change; it did not invent that rivalry.[8]

Necessity, functionality, embeddedness

From what I have said, it can be seen that while the charges laid against nationalism apply with force to specific doctrines and particular movements, they often either miss the point or overstate the case in regard to 'nationalism-in-general'.

In conclusion I want to set out briefly three arguments which together suggest both a qualified defence of the plural order of nations and the unlikelihood of any early supersession of nations and nationalism. These arguments are: that nationalism is politically necessary; that national identity is socially functional; and that the nation is historically embedded.

(1) In chapter 4, I discussed the importance of nationalism for a modern plural world order. Given the plurality of recognized states since at least 1648, the introduction of nationalist principles since 1789 can be seen as underpinning, enlarging and humanizing the political order of the interstate system by basing it on cultural and historical criteria, that is, on the prior existence of historic culture-communities. These are popular communities whose culture and traditions ex-

press their aspirations as a community, and for whom nationalism seeks a place in the distribution of world power. That is why nationalisms so frequently strive against the existing states and interstate order, so as to make room for submerged and unrecognized culture-communities in a world of national states. Moreover, nationalists contend that each state in the plural world order should possess a distinctive political personality based on a separate and unique culture-community or nation. This became evident to others besides nationalists once the powers of the monarch had been eroded and transferred to the sovereign people. The question 'who are the people?' became unavoidable, and nationalism provided a general answer in the shape of a historic community of public culture, which the nationalists were helping to adapt and complete. Soon no other legitimation for an order of plural sovereigns, and no other source of political power, became acceptable.

It follows that nations and nationalisms remain political necessities because (and for as long as) they alone can ground the interstate order in the principles of popular sovereignty and the will of the people, however defined. Only nationalism can secure the assent of the governed to the territorial units to which they have been assigned, through a sense of collective identification with historic culture-communities in their 'homelands'. As long as any global order is based on a balance of competing states, so long will the principle of nationality provide the only widely acceptable legitimation and focus of popular mobilization. Since there is little sign that the competition of states, even in Europe, is being superseded by some completely new political order, the likelihood of the nation which forms the *raison d'être* of the state and its community of will being transcended remains remote. Even if a number of states were to pool their sovereignties and even if their national communities were to agree to federate within a single political framework, the nation and its nationalism would long remain the only valid focus and constituency for ascertaining the popular will. Elsewhere there is little sign of such federative activity, and a pluralist world of nations and national states remains the only safeguard against imperial tyranny.

(2) National identity, as opposed to other kinds of collective identity, is pre-eminently functional for modernity, being suited to the needs of a wide variety of social groups and individuals in the modern epoch. This is not primarily because nationalism is functional for an industrial society which requires armies of mobile, literate citizens for its effective operation. Rather, the myths, memories, symbols and ceremonies of nationalism provide the sole basis for such social cohesion and political action as modern societies, with their often heterogenous social and ethnic composition and varied aims, can muster. Nationalism is an ideology of historic territory, and it concentrates the energies of individuals and groups within a clearly demarcated 'homeland', in which all citizens are deemed to be brothers and sisters and to which they therefore 'belong'. By rehearsing the rites of fraternity in a political community in its homeland at periodic intervals, the nation communes with and worships itself, making its citizens feel the power and warmth of their collective identification and inducing in them a heightened self-awareness and social reflexivity.[9]

As a result, individual members come to perceive the social functions of their dependence on the nation, including such collective needs as the preservation of their community's irreplaceable culture values, the rediscovery of its authentic roots, the celebration and emulation of its exemplars of heroic virtue, the re-creation of feelings of fraternity and kinship and the mobilization of citizens for common goals. From these needs, so often the themes of communal exhortations, flow the rituals and ceremonies, customs and festivals, traditions and symbols which commemorate and celebrate the nation in every generation. Their common purpose is to arouse in the citizens a national consciousness and generate a national will, and they achieve these ends through mass, public displays and vivid imagery. Though some brave souls may oppose particular national regimes, most of the citizens have shown themselves all too willing to participate in and celebrate the rites of the nation and accept the received narratives and myths of national identity. Defections have always been minimal and most members to this day continue to identify with the ideal version of the nation portrayed by nationalism.[10]

Moreover, the sense of national identity is often powerful enough to engender a spirit of self-sacrifice on behalf of the nation in many, if not most, of its citizens. This is especially true of crises and wartime. Here one can witness the degree to which most citizens are prepared to endure hardships and make personal sacrifices 'in defence of the nation', to the point of laying down their lives willingly, often in vast numbers, as occurred in several of the combatant countries during both World Wars. Such self-sacrifice on this scale is unimaginable for any other kind of collective cultural identity and community in our epoch, except perhaps for a few religious communities, and it is the singular power of the nation in eliciting mass sacrifice that has made it so often the object of unscrupulous demagogues. By the same token, the nation has become the main vehicle of warfare and national identity the chief justification for participation in lethal combat. England and Ireland; France and Germany; Greece and Turkey; Israel and the Arabs; India and Pakistan; the Khmers and Vietnamese: the roll-call of ethno-national antagonisms in the modern epoch recalls how wars have strengthened national consciousness and how the mobilization of nations has changed the nature of warfare for ever.[11]

All this in itself is insufficient to predict the persistence of national identity. As has been often demonstrated, the functionality of an institution or ideology is no proof of its continued presence or influence. At the same time, the many functions that national identity continues to perform need to be taken into account in assessing the vitality of contemporary nationalism.

(3) As I have argued throughout, the nation is historically embedded. It is the modern heir and transformation of the much older and commoner *ethnie* and as such gathers to itself all the symbols and myths of pre-modern ethnicity. Combining these pre-modern ties and sentiments with the explosive modern charge of popular sovereignty and mass, public culture, nationalism has created a unique modern drama of national liberation and popular mobilization in an ancestral homeland. The older myths of ethnic election – the belief in the conditional chosenness of certain communities whose divine privileges depended on the continued performance of their duties – have not withered away. Nationalism has given them a new lease of life, inspiring a yearning for collective regeneration in the homeland and for salvation of the national elect provided they repossess their authentic identity and ancestral soil, as has been so vividly demonstrated by Zionism and Armenian nationalism.[12]

There are other examples of the historical embeddedness of the nation in much older ethnic frameworks. While the *idea* of the nation can be disembedded, generalized and transferred to milieux where there is no obvious historic *ethnie* or ancestral homeland, as in such heterogenous immigrant island communities as Trinidad and Mauritius, most actual nations have derived their power from their popular and political links with much older ethnic communities and identities. This has allowed nationalists to return, rediscover and reappropriate traditional customs, symbols and ceremonies, such as the Welsh *Eisteddfodau*, which despite several adaptations and changes, broadly followed the main lines of the medieval Welsh bardic contests which had gradually died out in the sixteenth century but had survived in the popular consciousness in the local 'almanack *eisteddfodau*'.

Alternatively, religious elites may preserve older forms of celebration, such as the Jewish agricultural festivals of ancient Palestine which were kept from year to year by increasingly urbanized diaspora communities, to be revived as national festivals by the early Zionists on their return to Israel.[13]

Heroes and sagas have also been reappropriated by modern nationalism for its own ends. Muhammad and Moses have ceased to be prophets and servants of God, and have become national leaders *par excellence*; mythological bards like Oisin (Ossian) and Vainamoinen have become exemplars of ancient Irish and Finnish national wisdom; the heroes of the *Ramayana* have become prototypes of Indian national resistance. What is of interest here is not the uses to which these ancient exemplars have been put by often unscrupulous leaders, but the fervour of the believing masses. The power of their identification with an ethnic past with its heroic myths and legends, symbols and values, is vital to the success of the nationalist enterprise. It is also decisive for the content of the ensuing nationalism. The ethnic past sets limits to the manipulations of the elites and provides the ideals for the restored nation and its destiny. In this way, the nation remains embedded in a past that shapes its future as much as any present global trends. The 'blocking presentism' of so much latterday analysis should not blind one to the continuing if sometimes hidden power of the nation's lineage, and to the persistence of particular ethnic ties and sentiments in which the nation is so often embedded.[14]

But it is not simply the embeddedness of the nation as it is known today that is at issue; its destiny too owes its meaning and direction to successive interpretations of the ethnic past. It is this linking of ethno-history with national destiny that works most powerfully to uphold and preserve a world of nations. The modern nation has become what ethno-religious communities were in the past: communities of history and destiny that confer on mortals a sense of immortality through the judgement of posterity, rather than through divine judgement in an afterlife.

This ability to satisfy a more general craving for immortality marks out nationalism from other ideologies and belief-systems of the modern world. In some areas, it has enabled nationalism to ally itself with world religions like Islam or Buddhism; in others to substitute itself for crumbling traditions. In both cases, however, what sets out as essentially secular ideology and symbolism of culture and politics reveals a transcendental dimension, one that raises the individual above the earthly round and out of immediate time. In this sense, nationalism can be regarded as a 'religion surrogate' and the nation as a continuation, but also a transformation, of pre-modern ethno-religious community.[15]

Conclusion

I have argued that, despite the capacity of nationalisms to generate widespread terror and destruction, the nation and nationalism provide the only realistic socio-cultural framework for a modern world order. They have no rivals today. National identity too remains widely attractive and effective and is felt by many people to satisfy their needs for cultural fulfilment, rootedness, security and fraternity. Many people are still prepared to answer the call of the nation and lay down their lives for its cause. Finally, nations are linked by the chains of memory, myth and symbol to that widespread and enduring type of community, the *ethnie*, and this is what gives them their unique character and their profound hold over the feelings and imaginations of so many people.

None of this is to deny 'the dark side of nationalism', its capacity for division, destabilization and destruction. What has to be explained is the ubiquitous power of nations and nationalism in a global world, and this can be done only if one grasps their ethno-historical foundations and the manner in which modern trends have revitalized and have been shaped by persisting ethnic ties.

In the light of all these considerations, it would be folly to predict an early supersession of nationalism and an imminent transcendence of the nation. Both remain indispensable elements of an interdependent world and a mass-communications culture. For a global culture seems unable to offer the qualities of collective faith, dignity and hope that only a 'religion surrogate', with its promise of a territorial culture-community across the generations, can provide. Over and beyond any political or economic benefits that ethnic nationalism can confer, it is this promise of collective but terrestrial immortality, outfacing death and oblivion, that has helped to sustain so many nations and national states in an era of unprecedented social change and to renew so many ethnic minorities that seemed to be doomed in an era of technological uniformity and corporate efficiency.

Notes

1 See A. D. Smith (1991 and 1990a).

INTRODUCTION

1 For the concepts of 'globalization' and 'time-space compression', see Featherstone (1990, esp. Robertson).
2 For the breakdown of nations, see Kohr (1957); and McNeill (1986) for an updated version.
3 Carr (1945) and Deutsch (1966) remain the sources of such modernism, as applied to nations. For a more general statement of the revolutions of modernity, see Giddens (1991).
4 This view goes back to Shils (1957) and was elaborated by Geertz (1963).

CHAPTER 1   A COSMOPOLITAN CULTURE?

1 Hobsbawm (1990, 163): Hobsbawm sees the apogee of nationalism in the early twentieth century, which betrays a periodizing historical view in line with earlier historians' accounts of nationalism; on which see Snyder (1954).
2 Ibid., 164, which is in line with classical Marxist attacks on the small nationalities' movements of Eastern Europe; see Cummins (1980).
3 Ibid., 166–7: Hobsbawm cites the growing ethnic mix of

Canada's large cities, in connection with Quebecois nationalism.

4 Ibid., 168–9.

5 Ibid., 173, an argument made in the context of a wistful survey of the ways in which communist regimes in Yugoslavia and the Soviet Union limited the 'disastrous effects of nationalism' within their borders.

6 Ibid., 177 – an argument which assumes a scenario that envisages every ethno-national candidate becoming a sovereign nation-state. This is a straw man. Not only is such a scenario impracticable, it has never even been sought as a global programme. What has happened is that particular *ethnies* or leaders thereof have clamoured for national status; once again, nationalism, the disembedded ideology, has been dependent on specific pre-existing ethnic ties.

7 Ibid., 181–3; cf. Kedourie (1960). In his Introduction, Hobsbawm lists a number of scholarly advances in the study of nationalism since the 1970s, which overlooks the many earlier achievements of such historians as Carlton Hayes, Louis Snyder, Boyd Shafer and Hans Kohn. See A. D. Smith (1992b).

8 Ibid., ch. 1; For the views of Marx and Engels on current European nationalisms, see Davis (1967).

9 Carr (1945); Kohn (1967); Smelser (1968); cf. also Deutsch (1966) and Breuilly (1982). Liberal evolutionism is common to these and other analysts, despite their theoretical and disciplinary differences.

10 See Nairn (1977, ch. 5) for the distinction between objective material reality and romantic subjectivism; for the cultural approaches among scholars, see Meadwell (1989).

11 For this principle, see Gellner (1983, ch. 1); for critiques of such unidimensional readings of nationalism, see Orridge (1981) and Hutchinson (1987).

12 On the post-war resurgence of ethno-nationalism in the West, see Esman (1977) and Williams (1982a); for some causes of ethnic secession and irredentism in Asia and Africa, see Horowitz (1985, ch. 6). Horowitz emphasizes the role of poverty and backwardness of groups and regions. There is, however, considerable evidence that more 'advanced' groups in

wealthier regions are also liable to seek greater autonomy and even to secede from uncongenial polyethnic states.

13 On these international conditions and dimensions of nationalism, see Hinsley (1973) and Wiberg (1983). The right of national self-determination in the UN Charter has been restricted to liberation movements from imperial and colonial rule, but there are signs (e.g. from Slovaks, Slovenes, Croatians, Palestinians) that it may be widened to include ethnic movements of self-determination from national states.

14 For Marxist versions, see Davis (1967) and Connor (1984a).

15 A thesis advanced by Sklair (1991); cf. Mandel (1975). For the concept of 'disembedding', see Giddens (1991).

16 For a critique of accounts of media imperialism and the global impact of the mass media, see Schlesinger (1987).

17 This is argued by Richmond (1984) in the context of a wider shift from an industrial to a 'post-industrial' service type of society, under the aegis of capitalism and communism. For social movements as interpersonal protest networks, see Melucci (1989). See more generally A. D. Smith (1990a).

18 On cultural imperialism and national autonomy, see Tomlinson (1991, esp. ch. 3).

19 For a fuller description, on which this section draws, see A. D. Smith (1990b).

20 The ambivalent and hybrid character of modern Western national identities, and their redefinition in terms of the Other – in this case, minorities, immigrants and the ex-colonized – is highlighted by Bhabha (1990, ch. 16).

21 For medieval Islam and Christianity as ethno-religious civilizations, which contain smaller ethnic identities, and provide them with symbolic resources, see Armstrong (1982, ch. 3). On centralized bureaucratic empires generally, see Eisenstadt (1963) and Mann (1986, vol. I); for sacred realms, see Anderson (1983, ch. 2).

22 See Gouldner (1979) for the distinction between the humanistic and technical intelligentsia.

23 Weber (1947, 176) for this phrase.

24 The concept of 'invented traditions' is analysed and illustrated in Hobsbawm and Ranger (1983); cf. Schlesinger (1987) for the

differential national reception and understanding of television imagery.

25 Tomlinson (1991, ch. 3); cf. the discussion of globalization and pluralization in Arnason (1990).

26 See also Hobsbawm (1977).

27 This idea is associated with the economist Friedrich List. Its political parallel was Hegel's theory of the 'historyless peoples', the idea that only great nations which had possessed states of their own in the past could build states of their own in the future. See, for example, Kahan (1968); Rosdolsky (1964).

28 See the implicit critique of Hobsbawm (1977) by Warren (1980), for whom political independence is a prerequisite for capitalist economic development. The vast differences in size of population and extent of territory of recognized nations must also be remembered: from Iceland's 250,000 to Germany's 80,000,000 and Russia's 130,000,000, not to mention India and China.

29 This was also true in the past; see the analysis in Argyle (1976) of ethnic minority nationalisms in the Habsburg empire. For today's movements, see, for example, Tiryakian and Rogowski (1985); cf. Hall (1979).

30 On the need to keep these domains separate, see Mouzelis (1990). For a vigorous critique of the widespread tendency to explain ethnic nationalism in terms of economic processes, see Connor (1984b).

CHAPTER 2   THE MODERNIST FALLACY

1 See Lowenthal (1985); and for some reasons as to why modernity constitutes a revolution, see Giddens (1991).

2 See Okamura (1981).

3 For this 'social boundary' approach, see Barth (1969, Introduction); in a sense, Barth's is not a pure instrumentalism, let alone situationalism, since he believes that, though they are made and remade by continuous transactions across the boundaries, ethnic identities are in some sense pre-existing and 'out there' in terms of durable social boundary processes reinforced by symbolic 'border guards'; see Jenkins (1988). For an instrumental

approach that recognizes the importance of 'affect', the emotional properties of ethnicity, alongside social interest, see Bell (1975).

4 See Brass (1979) for an application of this elite approach to the Muslims of North India.

5 See Cobban (1964, ch. 4) for Rousseau and the French Revolutionary doctrines; and Reiss (1955) for German political Romanticism.

6 Van den Berghe (1979); for a general account of socio-biology, see Badcock (1991).

7 The argument in Geertz (1963) which draws on Shils (1957) is that members and participants endow ethnic ties with a primordial quality; primordiality is a matter of attribution, it does not inhere in its cognitive objects; it is a power conferred on its objects by human beings; cf. also Stack (1986, Introduction).

8 For these arguments, see Brass (1979 and 1980). McNeill (1986, ch. 1) argues that civilization requires specialized labour and therefore has always had polyethnic hierarchies.

9 See V. Reynolds (1980) for a critique of socio-biology. For a 'rational choice' model, see Hechter (1987 and 1988). Geertz's version of primordiality has been severely criticized by Eller and Coughlan (1993), and defended by Grosby (1994).

10 See Grosby (1991) for a learned and telling application of the Geertzian approach to ancient Israelite religion and nationality.

11 On the persistence of Punic culture, see Moscati (1973, 168–9); on the gradual Islamization of Iran and the Persian renaissance, see Frye (1966, ch. 6); the fundamental kinship nature and 'blood' metaphor of ethnicity is briefly discussed in Nash (1989) and underlined by Connor (1993).

12 For earlier 'perennialist' analyses of nationality in the ancient and early medieval worlds, see Koht (1947) and Levi (1965).

13 See, *inter alia*, Kedourie (1960), Gellner (1964, ch. 7) and Nairn (1977, ch. 2); cf. Anderson (1983) and Hobsbawm (1990) for the greater emphasis on the socially 'constructed' nature of nations and nationalisms. The differences between their analyses are, in fact, less important than their shared basic commitment to 'modernism'.

14 A line of analysis that goes back to Cobban (1945, ch. 2); see Tilly (1975, Introduction and Conclusion).

15 For the view that nationalism represents a specious response to the alienation engendered by the rift between the state and modern society, see Breuilly (1982, Conclusion). For the idea that nationalism complements psychologically the reflexive nature of the modern state, affording a locus of trust and cooperation, see Giddens (1985, ch. 8, and 1991).

16 Gellner (1983) is more materialist and functionalist than his earlier theory (1964, ch. 7); it lays less emphasis on language and more on the links between mass public education, high culture and industrialism.

17 See Seton-Watson (1977, chs. 2–3); for the rise of nationalism in sixteenth-century England, see Greenfeld (1992, ch. 2). For earlier debates about nationalism in the Middle Ages, see Tipton (1972). For the existence of elite national sentiments in medieval Europe, see S. Reynolds (1984) and Guenée (1985, ch. 3).

18 For 'nation-building', see Deutsch and Foltz (1963); for a trenchant critique, see Connor (1972). On secession and irredentism in Africa and Asia, see Horowitz (1985, ch. 6).

19 For a 'rational choice' model of secession, see Hechter (1992); cf. Meadwell (1989). For the self-sacrificing components of nationalism, see Anderson (1983).

20 Hobsbawm (1990, ch. 2); but even he concedes that later Russian nationalism may owe something to the 'proto-national' communities attached to Tsar and Church; on which, see Cherniavsky (1975). See also Robinson, in Taylor and Yapp (1979), for a critique of the elite approach, as applied by Brass (1974) to the Muslims of North India.

21 Seton-Watson (1977). D. E. Smith (1974) gives examples of the religious revival, while A. D. Smith (1989) stresses the role of ethnic cores. One should also add that the role of religion in the past continues to shape many present ethnic conflicts and national profiles; Ireland, Poland, Serbia and Greece are obvious examples in Europe, but it can be argued that the cooler response of Scandinavian peoples to 'Europe' owes something to their Protestant suspicion of a Catholic-led continent.

22 For political myth, see Tudor (1972); for the myth of the

'modern nation', see A. D. Smith (1988).

23 For these pioneers and models, see Bendix (1966).

24 On the differential timing of nationalism around the world, see Orridge (1980).

25 For the earlier French attitudes, see Benthem van den Berghe (1966). For the revision of received traditions in French history teaching which was based on the various Lavisse textbooks, see Citron (1988); and for persisting regionalism in France, see Braudel (1989).

26 The social composition of Quebecois nationalism is analysed in Pinard and Hamilton (1984).

27 For a comparison with Basque nationalism, see Payne (1971); and see Conversi (1994) for a more detailed analysis.

28 For American providential nationalism, see Kohn (1957a) and Tuveson (1968).

29 The persistence of nationalism in Ireland into the twentieth century is analysed in Lyons (1979) and Hutchinson (1987); for religion and nationalism in post-war Poland, see Chrypinski (1989). For Norway, see Mitchison (1980) on earlier nationalist trends; and for more recent developments, including scepticism, even resistance, to the European Community, see Waever (1992).

30 On such neo-fascism, see Wilkinson (1983) and Husbands (1991).

31 For a fuller exposition of these pre-modern influences, see A. D. Smith (1986a, ch. 8).

32 Steinberg (1976) gives a vivid account of the complexities of Swiss national identity.

33 For a full account of the historical formation of Swiss national identity and unity, see Im Hof (1991), who dates the process of national formation back to the late fifteenth century.

34 For general histories, see Kohn (1957b) and Thurer (1970).

35 See the 'modernist' Swiss history of Fahrni (1983), which downplays the significance of the foundation myth and of ethnic ties; see also Kreis (1991) for a social constructionist approach to the Swiss national myth of 1291, interpreted as a nationalist artefact of the late nineteenth century.

CHAPTER 3   AN ETHNO-NATIONAL REVIVAL?

1 For the origins of these movements, see Mayo (1974); on the Scottish movement, see Hanham (1969); for the Basque and Catalan movements, see Payne (1971).

2 Western neo-nationalisms have produced a large literature: see *inter alia* Esman (1977), Williams (1982a) and Tiryakian and Rogowski (1985).

3 For the metaphor of the Sleeping Beauty, see Minogue (1967a); for images of national reawakening, rebirth and renewal, see Pearson (1993).

4 For a striking perennialist statement, see Fishman (1980). A more complex position is adumbrated by Armstrong (1982, ch. 1), where ethnicity and nationality are regarded as interchangeable and closely allied, as sets of perceptions, attitudes and sentiments, with both religious and class identities; but a historic watershed – the introduction of nationalism – distinguishes nations before 1775–1815 and those after this period (Armstrong 1992a).

5 Johnson (1992) has raised some of these issues concerning the exhibition catalogue *The Making of England* (see Webster and Backhouse 1991), whose Historical Introduction by Nicolas Brooks opens thus:

> The Anglo-Saxons, whose artistic, technological and cultural achievements in the seventh, eighth and ninth centuries are displayed in this exhibition, were the true ancestors of the English of today. At the time these works were produced, there were several rival Anglo-Saxon kingdoms, each of which had its own dynasty, its own aristocracy and its own separate traditions and loyalties. Spoken English already showed wide regional variations of dialect. None the less the Anglo-Saxons had a sense that they were one people (p. 9).

6 For the view that the nation and nationalism are the central issues which define the contents of modernity, see Greenfeld (1992, ch. 1); see also Armstrong (1992a). These features of the ancient Jewish commonwealth are delineated in Mendels

(1992), who nevertheless makes it clear that his use of the concept of nationality in the ancient world is more akin to *ethnie* and ethnicity than to modern nations and nationalisms.

7 There is a special problem relating to ancient city-states, which might well be described as precocious, if small-scale, nations. Thus the size of ancient Athens was about the same as modern Iceland (*c.* 250,000). On the other hand, only the 30,000 adult male Athenians were citizens; metics, women and slaves were excluded. Moreover, from a nationalist standpoint, they lacked the key component of cultural individuality (rather than homogeneity); Athenian culture was a variant of a wider Ionian ethnic, and still wider Hellenic cultural, network. See Alty (1982) and Finley (1986, ch. 7). For the idea that nations and nationalisms are exclusively mass, and hence twentieth-century, phenomena, see Connor (1990).

8 For the latter, see Kedourie (1960). For citizenship and the modern nation, see Bendix (1964) and Breuilly (1982, Conclusion). For federal nations, see Birch (1989).

9 For a sustained attack on the doctrine of nationalism, see Kedourie (1960); but cf. A. D. Smith (1971, ch. 7) and chapter 6 of this book. For the view that pre-modern 'agro-literate' societies, with their rigid elite-mass divisions, allowed no scope for nations and nationalism, see Gellner (1983, ch. 2). For the earlier development of ideas of national character, see the scholarly study of Kemilainen (1964).

10 For the growth of the interstate system in Western Europe, see Cobban (1945) and Tilly (1975).

11 The territorial 'homeland' component of nations is explored by A. D. Smith and Williams (1983).

12 For definitions of the 'nation', see *inter alia* Deutsch (1966, chs 1 and 4), Connor (1978) and A. D. Smith (1991, ch. 1).

13 Fuller discussions of *ethnies* and ethnicity can be found in Schermerhorn (1970), de Vos and Romanucci (1975), Armstrong (1982) and A. D. Smith (1986a, ch. 2).

14 On Breton nationalism, see Berger (1977) and Beer (1977); early Catalan and Basque nationalisms are compared in Conversi (1990); for a brief history of Serbs and Croats, see Singleton (1985) and in more detail Jelavich (1983, esp. ch. 6).

15 For a fuller exploration of the problem of pre-modern nations,

see A. D. Smith (1994), in which the proposed criteria are less restrictive than those employed by Connor (1990).

16 For differences in types of pre-modern *ethnies*, see Armstrong (1982, chs 1, 3 and 7) and A. D. Smith (1986a, ch. 4).

17 For a striking myth of ethnic election feeding an early modern nationalism in the Netherlands, see Schama (1987, ch. 2); cf. also Kohn (1940) for a Puritan English nationalism of the ethnic elect. On these ethnic election myths in general, see A. D. Smith (1992a).

18 The general argument about the effects of core exploitation on peripheral ethno-regions in Britain is documented by Hechter (1975). For specific cases, see Stone (1979).

19 For a penetrating analysis of ethno-regional variations in European states, see Orridge (1982). For Eastern European patterns of ethnic subordination and nationalisms, see Sugar and Lederer (1969).

20 See Hechter (1975), and the revision to his position to allow for Scotland's 'segmental division of labour', in Hechter and Levi (1979). For critical applications to other industrial peripheries of the concept of 'internal colonialism', see the essays in Stone (1979); cf. A. D. Smith (1981a, ch. 2).

21 For diaspora communities, see Armstrong (1976).

22 For political myth, see Tudor (1972); for the study of myth in general, see Kirk (1973). Such political myths or *mythomoteurs* are central to the analysis of ethnic identity in medieval Islam and Christendom by Armstrong (1982). For a radical critique of ethno-history and myth, see the introduction to Tonkin, McDonald and Chapman (1989).

23 For some examples, see A. D. Smith (1984).

24 Two examples of the recovery of obscured and ill-documented ethnic pasts on behalf of communities overshadowed by more powerful or more culturally advanced neighbours are provided by the Slovaks and the Ukrainians; on which see the perceptive essays by Paul (1985) and Saunders (1993).

25 On which, see Armstrong (1982, ch. 7) and A. D. Smith (1986a, ch. 5).

26 For the artistic pilgrimage to Brittany in the later nineteenth century in search of a primitive and pure ethnic religiosity, see Royal Academy of Arts (1979, especially under Emile Bernard).

The compilation of the *Kalevala* by Lönnrot in 1835 is fully documented in Branch (1985, Introduction) and discussed by Honko (1985).

27 For Herder's ideas, see Berlin (1976); for Lord Shaftesbury's influence, see Macmillan (1986).

28 For a critical appraisal of the relationship between language and nationalism, see Edwards (1985, ch. 2); the role of philologists, grammarians and lexicographers in mass-mobilizing European nationalisms is emphasized by Anderson (1983, ch. 5).

29 For Romantic music and nationalism, see Raynor (1976); on the national motifs in the music of Sibelius, see Layton (1985) and in the music of Elgar, Crump (1986). For history painting and nationalism in Europe, see Rosenblum (1967, ch. 2), and more generally, A. D. Smith (1993a). For modern Latin American painting and images of national identity, see Ades (1989, chs 7 and 9).

30 The Afrikaner celebration of the Covenant and the Battle of Blood River in 1838 is the subject of considerable debate, academic as well as political. The impact of the ceremonial oath and ritual is assessed by Breuilly (1982, ch. 16), who regards nationalist ceremonial and symbolism as the most powerful aspect of the phenomenon. The historical basis of the myths of the Voortrekkers and the Covenant is dissected by Thompson (1985), who concludes that the Covenant and its ceremonies were largely Paul Kruger's invention in the early 1880s.

31 For the heroization of the ethnic past, especially in India, see Kedourie (1971, Introduction); for this process among the Arabs, see Sharabi (1970) and Kedourie (1992, ch. 6). The use of the golden age of Ulster by Irish nationalists is explored by Lyons (1979) and Hutchinson (1987, chs 3–4).

32 On the national variations of Romanticism, see Porter and Teich (1988). For the view that nationalism, the most Romantic and subjectivist of ideologies and sentiments, is nevertheless explicable in terms of uneven capitalist development, see Nairn (1977, chs 2 and 9).

33 For these 'volkisch' writers and their glorification of the soil, see Mosse (1964); the conservative religious nationalism of the

Slavophiles is carefully analysed by Thaden (1964).

34 See the excellent account of Codreanu's movement in E. Weber (1966).

35 For recent Russian nationalism, see Dunlop (1985) and Pospielovsky (1989).

36 For these movements, see Williams (1982a); for some general explanations of Western neo-nationalisms, see Allardt (1979) and A. D. Smith (1981a, chs 1 and 9).

37 For the Breton movement, see Berger (1977) and Beer (1977); for the Welsh Language Society and Welsh nationalism, see Williams (1977) and (1982b); for the Basques, Medhurst (1982).

38 For the minority middleman theory, see Bonacich (1973) and the summary of such theories in Zenner (1991, ch. 1). For a critical appraisal, see Horowitz (1985, ch. 2).

39 Connor (1984b); for supporting historical evidence, see A. D. Smith (1971, ch. 6).

40 For the prominence of intellectuals and professionals or intelligentsia in nationalist movements, see Kedourie (1971, Introduction), Gella (1976), A. D. Smith (1981a, chs 5–6) and Anderson (1983); for a critical assessment, see Breuilly (1982, ch. 15). Hroch (1985) has advanced a three-stage social explanation of stateless nationalisms in Eastern Europe, which gives a prominent role to ethnic intellectuals and intelligentsia in stages (A) and (B).

41 Gouldner (1979) charts the division between the two wings of the intelligentsia, the humanistic and technical, and sketches the transition from the former to the latter; for some firm evidence of the prominence of the intelligentsia in the Quebecois case, see Pinard and Hamilton (1984).

42 For the background to Scottish nationalism, see Hanham (1969) and Nairn (1977, ch. 2); for the rise of the SNP, see Webb (1977), Brand (1978) and MacIver (1982).

43 For the rise of Welsh nationalism, see K. Morgan (1982); for the revival of Welsh cultural traditions, including the *Eisteddfodau*, see P. Morgan (1983).

44 For a detailed analysis of the rise and current revival of Catalan nationalism, see Conversi (1994).

45 This dual loyalty in the West, to the territorial national state and the ethnic nation, and the conditions that have made such dual loyalties possible, are analysed by A. D. Smith (1986b) and Birch (1989). For a historical study of the rise of a specifically British nationalism in the eighteenth century, see Colley (1992).

46 For this distinction, see Kohn (1967, ch. 7); cf. Plamenatz (1976). See the critiques in A. D. Smith (1971, ch. 8) and Hutchinson (1987, ch. 1). For the declining Soviet Union, see G. E. Smith (1989).

47 On the Soviet nationalities, see especially G. E. Smith (1990) and Bremmer and Taras (1993). For the revival of East European nationalisms, see Ramet (1989), Vardys (1989) and Glenny (1990). For an explanation of the differential development of East European nationalism, in terms of stages of its evolution, see Gellner (1992).

48 For the role of the Catholic Church in recent Polish nationalism, see Chrypinski (1989).

49 For the rise of Slovak nationalism, see Brock (1976) and Paul (1985); for the later relations between Czechs and Slovaks, see Glenny (1990, 137–44).

50 For the history of the area, see Jelavich (1983). For a theory which emphasizes the 'security dilemma' between Serbs and Croats arising out of anarchical conditions such as the collapse of states where group action seems threatening, especially when reinforced by vivid memories of group conflict, see Posen (1993).

51 For the early South Slav movements, see Stavrianos (1961) and, for a critical view of the transition from Orthodoxy to nationalism, see Kitromilides (1989).

52 See Gouldner (1979) and n. 40 above, as well as Shils (1960).

53 For the religious roots of the Islamic revolution in Iran, see Keddie (1981); and see Halliday (1979) for the wider geopolitical conditions. For Sri Lanka, see Roberts (1993); on Orthodoxy in Russia, see Pospielovsky (1989).

54 See D. E. Smith (1974) for the mass-mobilizing potential of religious traditions; see also Banuazizi and Weiner (1986). For a striking example of Islamic and Christian revivalism in present-day Nigeria, see Igwara (1993).

CHAPTER 4   THE CRISIS OF THE NATIONAL STATE

1 See Connor (1972) and Wiberg (1983); cf. also the distinctions in Tivey (1980).

2 For the 'parallel society', see Balandier (1954); cf. J. H. Kautsky (1962, Introduction). For the pattern of social relations in Eastern Europe, see Sugar (1980).

3 For these ancient aristocracies, see Moscati (1962), Cook (1983) and Mann (1986, ch. 5).

4 On Tudor Britain, see Corrigan and Sayer (1985, ch. 2) and for French and Spanish religious motives, see Armstrong (1982, ch. 3).

5 For French linguistic centralization, see Rickard (1974); for eighteenth-century English, and British, nationalisms, see Newman (1987) and Colley (1992).

6 For enfranchisement, see Bendix (1964); for the rise of centralized administration and professional warfare, see Tilly (1975) and Giddens (1985).

7 See pp. 56–7 for this definition; for a rather different agenda of 'nation-building', see Deutsch and Foltz (1963). The social communication model of Deutsch emphasizes the volume of messages, and the mechanisms of their transmission; but it fails to specify the content of the shared memories – of culture, community and homeland – transmitted across the generations, or to appreciate the power of symbols, myths and traditions embodied in customs, rituals and ceremonies.

8 For this emphasis on the crucial role of mass, standardized, public education systems in creating nations, see Gellner (1983, chs 3–4). For the case of the French Third Republic, see the classic study of E. Weber (1979); for the study of history textbooks from the 1880s to the 1980s, see Citron (1988); and for the inculcation of Greek ideals of physical fitness after the defeat by Prussia, see Leoussi (1992).

9 For Meiji Japan, see Lehmann (1982, ch. 8, esp. 259–65); for the role of the state in Islamic countries, see Rosenthal (1965); and on Egypt under Nasser, Vatikiotis (1969).

10 See Lerner (1958); cf. Nettl and Robertson (1968, part III).

11 On 'official' nationalism, see Anderson (1983, ch. 6). For the Mexican cultural renaissance and the muralists, see Franco

(1970) and Ades (1989, ch. 7).

12 For a penetrating account of the Thatcher government's attack on the professions in Britain, see Burrage (1992).

13 A structural element omitted in the otherwise perceptive analysis of Bhabha (1990, ch. 16); for an exploration of multiculturalism and its critics in Australia, see Castles et al. (1988, chs 6–7); cf. Kapferer (1988, chs 6–7, esp. the critique of Blainey).

14 This sundering of religion from ethnicity was achieved by Napoleon; see Hertzberg (1960, Introduction) on its consequences for Western Jewry. It was a product of the rising tide of French mass nationalism, and was quite different in kind from the impositions of the monarchical states on the Jews in the Middle Ages, including the mass expulsion of the Jews from a newly unified Catholic Spain in 1492; see Almog (1990, Introduction).

15 The 'great revolutions' occurred among peoples with ancient ethno-history, and nationalism soon suffused, if it did not partly motivate, the course of their revolutions; see for example C. Johnson (1969) on the nationalism of Maoist China and Gildea (1994) on Revolutionary France.

16 For some contemporary election myths, see Thompson (1985) on the Afrikaner Covenant; Kapferer (1988) on the Australian Anzac myth; O'Brien (1988) on the United States foundation and destiny myths; and Yoshino (1992) on the Japanese belief in their cultural uniqueness. For some dilemmas of Jewish and Israeli identity myths, see Segre (1980) and A. D. Smith (1992c).

17 For the ideal, as well as material, interests of the intellectuals and their national mission, see M. Weber (1947, 'The Nation') and A. D. Smith (1982).

18 For the way in which the Dreyfus Affair divided France, see Kedward (1965). On civic and ethnic nationalisms, see Ignatieff (1993).

19 See ch. 6 of this book; for such criticisms, see Porter (1965). For the Catalan counter-example, see Conversi (1990).

20 For the assimilation of Black elites and the cultural depreciation of the African, see W. H. Lewis (1965); for the French Republican treatment of the Jews, see Vital (1975).

21 This pressure of the periphery on the centre was analysed by

Eisenstadt (1965) and applied, with a new explanation, to Western states by Hechter and Levi (1979) and Orridge (1982).

22 For examples from colonial and post-colonial sub-Saharan Africa, see Markovitz (1977) and Young (1985). For the slogan 'L'Europe des Ethnies', see Heraud (1963). For a theory of nationalism arising from the needs of the state, see J. Snyder (1993).

23 For a review of contemporary ethnic nationalisms in the former Soviet Union and their prospects, see Armstrong (1992b); cf. the case studies in G. E. Smith (1990) and Bremmer and Taras (1993).

24 See Tilly (1975, Introduction and Conclusion).

25 For typologies of relations between states and *ethnies*, see Anderson, von der Mehden and Young (1967), Geertz (1963) and Brass (1985). For examples from south-east Asia, see Brown (1994).

26 On the causes of secessionist movements, see Horowitz (1985, ch. 6). On the conditions for their success, see Mayall (1990, ch. 4); cf. also Heraclides (1991).

27 For these fears, see Krol (1990) and Glenny (1990). For a fuller analysis, see A. D. Smith (1985).

28 For accounts of American messianic nationalism, see Kohn (1957a) and Tuveson (1968); on the 'symbolic ethnicity' of its third-generation white ethnics, see Gans (1979).

29 For these plural immigrant states, see Seton-Watson (1977, ch. 5); for their creole origins, see Anderson (1983, ch. 4). For the Canadian case, see Pinard and Hamilton (1982) and Laczko (1994). For multiculturalism and the Quebecois in Canada, see Birch (1989) and Meadwell (1989).

30 For the reaction to Muslim immigrants in France of the *Front National*, see Husbands (1991). The United States, too, has witnessed an anti-Hispanic backlash, and in Australia there has been strong right-wing criticism of the policies of multi-culturalism and Asian immigration; see Castles et al. (1988). Britain has also seen strong opposition to Afro-Caribbean and Asian immigrants; see James (1989). For the contribution of women to the process of reconstructing ethnic and national boundaries, and the need to rethink conceptions of the nation to include women, see Yuval-Davis (1993); cf. Gutierrez (1995).

31 On Mazzini's Young Europe and Young Italy movements, see Mack Smith (1994, ch. 1); for some consequences of the right of national self-determination and secession today, see Beitz (1979, part II) and Mayall (1990, ch. 4).

32 See for example Kedourie (1960), Tivey (1980, Introduction and ch. 3), Breuilly (1982, Introduction), Giddens (1985, 116–21, 209–21) and Hobsbawm (1990, ch. 1).

33 For the varieties of Swiss cultural and political identification and cross-cutting ties, see Warburton (1976) and Steinberg (1976, ch. 2).

34 See Zartmann (1963) for the concept of 'state-nation' – a state seeking to forge a nation – in Africa and Asia; on the influence of British and French colonialism and nationalisms in Africa, see Crowder (1968), and for the influence of territorial boundaries on the ethnic politics of Africa and Asia, see Horowitz (1985, ch. 2).

CHAPTER 5   SUPRA- OR SUPER-NATIONALISM?

1 See Renan (1882).

2 See Merritt and Rokkan (1966).

3 For a forthright statement of the dominance of transnational capitalism, see Sklair (1991).

4 For warfare and strategy in relation to national identities, see Marwick (1974), A. D. Smith (1981b) and Posen (1993).

5 For examples of the cultural success and political failure of 'Pan' movements, see Kohn (1960) on Pan-Slavism and Landau (1981) on Pan-Turkism.

6 For this slogan, see Mazrui (1966). For a comprehensive history of Pan-Africanism, see Geiss (1974).

7 On the limitations of economic nationalism, see Johnson (1968) and Mayall (1990, ch. 5).

8 See Gladwyn (1967) for the pro-European case; and Camps (1965) for the debates of the 1960s generated by Gaullism.

9 For the history of approaches to European integration, see Wallace (1990).

10 See ch. 2, nn. 2–3 above and A. D. Smith (1991, ch. 1).

11 For some reasons for the survival of these *ethnies*, see Armstrong (1982) and A. D. Smith (1986a, ch. 5); for the social boundary approach, see Barth (1969, Introduction).

12 For 'concentric circles of allegiance', see Coleman (1958).

13 For example, in ancient Greece, a common Hellenic culture did not produce a political union of the city-states, though some were induced to join the Lacedaemonian and Delian leagues led by Sparta and Athens (as well as later leagues). Conversely, political union in Belgium has not given rise to a shared culture. See Finley (1986, ch. 7) on ancient Greece, and Zolberg (1977) on Belgium.

14 See Davies (1982) for the history of Poland after the partitions; and Boyce (1982) for nineteenth-century Irish history. For another case, the Czechs and Slovaks, united together between the wars and under communism, but culturally separated, see Pynsent (1994, ch. 4).

15 For the German 'parallel', see Breuilly (1982, 65–82) and Hughes (1988, ch. 4); but it required Bismarck's policies and statesmanship to achieve sucess.

16 For the functionalist paradigm of European integration, see Haas (1964). See also Hoffman (1994).

17 For Scandinavian coolness, and nostalgia for 'Norden', see Waever (1992); the history of Pan-Europeanism is described by de Rougemont (1965) and Wallace (1990).

18 For medieval Western Europe, see Keen (1969); de Rougemont (1965) outlines the appeal of medieval Christendom as a model of European unity; cf. Krol (1990).

19 For the exclusion of heretics, lepers and Jews in the Middle Ages, see Moore (1987). On the modern European mosaic, see Krejci and Velimsky (1981). For the concept of a 'family of cultures', see A. D. Smith (1992d, esp. 70–1) on which this section draws.

20 On which, see Schlesinger (1992). There is the related problem of territorial demarcation of 'Europe'; this may help to account for the more developed European sensibility of people in the western half of the continent, protected as it is by oceans; and of people in the southern states seeking to distance themselves from cultural 'aliens' on the other side of the Mediterranean, despite the many links with North Africa, ancient and modern.

But why then the relative lack of European attachments among Scandinavians? The 'East' and the Balkans present fewer problems in this regard: their ambivalence is the product of their geopolitical and cultural indeterminacy, but the shifting borders of 'Europe' in the Orthodox lands reduce the overall sense of a compact historic European homeland. Is the European 'line' to be drawn at the Catholic–Orthodox border, the Christian–Muslim boundary, the Black Sea, the Caspian or the Urals (as de Gaulle put it)?

21 On the ideas of Michel Aflaq (a founder of the Syrian Ba'ath Party), see Binder (1964) and Kedourie (1971, Introduction). For the interpenetration of nationalist themes in nineteenth-century art within Europe, see A. D. Smith (1993a).

22 A Chassidic saying of the Baal Shem Tov. On Renan's analysis of memory and amnesia, see Gellner (1982). The American example of 'vernacular ancestralism' is discussed by Burrows (1982). For the general question of the role of ethnic memory, in relation to rival Greek traditions, see Just (1989) and A. D. Smith (1993b).

23 For the classical heritage in the Victorian era, see Jenkyns (1992) and Leoussi (1992).

24 For the medieval Christian 'myth-symbol complex', see Armstrong (1982, ch. 3); for patterns of European religion, see Martin (1978). The relationship between religion and national identity in Ireland and Yugoslavia is explored by Holmes (1982) and Alexander (1982). For the complex relations of religion and national consciousness in Eastern Europe, see Petrovich (1980) and Ramet (1989).

25 For recent research on Indo-European origins, see Mallory (1989); and the new theory put forward by Renfrew (1987). On European language divisions, see Armstrong (1982, ch. 8); for the antecedents of Nazi Aryanism, see Poliakov (1974).

26 On migration in the new Europe, see Miles (1993, esp. R. Fernhout: ' "Europe 1993" and its refugees', pp. 492–506); for the French situation and responses, see Miles and Singer-Kerel (1991).

27 On French support for Le Pen, see Husbands (1991); on minorities and national identity in Britain, see Samuel (1989, vol. II). On nationalism and fascism generally, see A. D. Smith

179

(1979a, ch. 3).

28 See Duroselle (1990), significantly entitled *Europe: A History of its Peoples*; see A. D. Smith (1992d) and Schlesinger (1992) for some criticisms.

29 For the national traditions of Romanticism, see Porter and Teich (1988); for national contrasts within the neo-classical tradition, see Rosenblum (1967) and A. D. Smith (1979b). For earlier 'great ages' and contributors to a 'European' history, see Duroselle (1990, chs 9–11), who seeks to highlight commonalities of experience, while recognizing the often partial nature of those experiences, and the deep internal differences between Europe's different cultural zones and peoples.

30 For this Western European predominance, see Wallace (1990). This assumes that (most of) Germany is Western and it overlooks important scientific, literary and artistic contributions of Eastern Europe and Russia.

31 See Atiyah (1968) and Ware (1984) for the Orthodox Church and Eastern Christianity; cf. also Ramet (1989, esp. essays on Yugoslavia, Romania and Bulgaria).

32 The statuary and monuments, ceremonies and emblems, of nationalism in Europe in the late nineteenth century are described by Hobsbawm in Hobsbawm and Ranger (1983, ch. 7); for a satirical tourist panorama of 'nationalist Europe', its relics and its shrines today, see Horne (1984).

33 On the liturgies of nationalism, see Mosse (1976); for its rites and ceremonies, see Breuilly (1982, ch. 16) and the detailed description of French Revolutionary patriotic celebrations, some of them organized by Jacques-Louis David, in Herbert (1972). American religio-nationalist ceremonies are described in O'Brien (1988). See also Schlesinger (1994).

34 For differing assessments of the background of the Macedonian conflict, see Alexander (1982) and Kofos (1990).

35 These kinship metaphors, and their 'primordial' power, are analysed by Horowitz (1985, ch. 6) and Connor (1993); cf. Grosby (1994).

36 The theme of a double attack on the national state, from above through European unity, and from below from the ethnic communities, goes back to the 1960s; see, for example, Heraud (1963).

37 For an early statement of these fears, see Galtung (1973); cf. the discussion in Schlesinger (1992).
38 The importance of such 'nostalgia' for idealized life-styles should not be underestimated; see Armstrong (1982, ch. 2). On the other hand, the vast increase in mass tourism and student exchanges, the dissemination of information about European developments by the media, and the spate of European art, music and film festivals, have made some of the younger generation more open to the idea of Europe and to the benefits of greater integration, though it is not clear whether such ideas are free from national biases and stereotypes, or how deep and long-lasting they may prove to be. See Schlesinger (1994).

CHAPTER 6   IN DEFENCE OF THE NATION

1 This chapter is based on a paper given to the Conference on 'Nations and Citizens' at the Centre for Philosophical Studies, King's College, London (1993), the latter part of which appears in Anthony D. Smith: 'Ties that Bind', *LSE Magazine* 5, 1, 1993, 8-11. See M. Weber (1947, 'The Nation'). Neuberger (1986, ch. 3) analyses the various criteria of national 'selfhood' in sub-Saharan Africa.
2 The use of plebiscites to ascertain the will of the people has raised difficult issues; see the trenchant critique in Kedourie (1960 and 1971); cf. also Breuilly (1982, Conclusion).
3 On the South Tyrol issue, see Doob (1964) and Katzenstein (1977). For an interesting discussion of national borders and political geography, in relation to the French 'hexagon', see E. Weber (1991, ch. 3).
4 But see the refutation in Kedourie (1960, 71-4). The most common distinction is that which stems from Hans Kohn, between an 'organic' doctrine found in Eastern Europe and a 'voluntarist' doctrine found in the West. But, while the distinction is important, it expresses two varieties of the same general belief-system, which frequently overlap in practice. For a discussion of various typologies of nationalism, see A. D. Smith (1971, ch. 8); cf. Gellner (1992).
5 For definitions of nationalism, see L. Snyder (1954) and Connor

(1978). For the definitions given here, see the fuller statements in A. D. Smith (1973, section 2, and 1991, ch. 4), and for that of the nation, chapter 3 above.

6 For such criticisms, see Minogue (1967b); cf. Porter (1965). They are partly answered by Miller (1993).

7 For Engels's observation, see Davis (1967, 22). German Romantic doctrines are described in Kohn (1965), Robson-Scott (1965) and Hughes (1988, ch. 2).

8 The 'insertion' of nationalism into a pre-existing order of states, first in Europe and then outside, is documented in Cobban (1945), Hinsley (1973) and Mayall (1990, chs 2–3). For arguments that suggest that destabilization (the breakdown of states) is the precondition rather than the effect of nationalism, see Snyder (1993) and Posen (1993).

9 It is odd that Durkheim, who was so concerned with social cohesion in modern societies, did not directly address the problem of nationalism; it may be that, like Weber, he had simply imbibed its assumptions, or that his views of social solidarity were indirectly (through the 'organic' German theorists of society) a product of a nationalist epoch. It was only during the First World War that his nationalism surfaced, but it is possible to read *The Elementary Forms of the Religious Life* (Fr. orig., 1912; Eng. trans., 1976), with its analogies between totemic and secular rites (of the French Revolution) and the need for 'religion' and periodic celebrations of the collective life in modern societies, as recognition of the centrality of the nation in the modern world. What is lacking, however, is a recognition of the myth of the homeland and the territorial dimension; see Mitchell (1931) and A. D. Smith (1983).

10 For the role of treason and loyalty, see Grodzins (1956); for national celebrations, see Eri and Jobbagyi (1989) on the Hungarian millennial celebrations of 1896, and more generally, Hobsbawm and Ranger (1983).

11 For the impact of the two World Wars on national cohesion, see Marwick (1974) and more generally, A. D. Smith (1981b). Themes of heroic self-sacrifice for the nation which were to the fore in neo-classical art, are explored in Rosenblum (1967, ch. 2) and A. D. Smith (1987, ch. 8).

12 This theme is more fully explored by A. D. Smith (1992a). For

Armenian and Zionist nationalism, see Walker (1980) and Almog (1987).

13 The contrast of 'formal' and 'informal nationalism' in Mauritius and Trinidad is analysed by Eriksen (1993); and the revival of the *Eisteddfodau* by P. Morgan (1983). For the urbanization of Mishnaic Judaism, see Neusner (1981), and for the revival of Jewish festivals by early Zionism, Hertzberg (1960).

14 For this 'blocking presentism', in relation to Yoruba ethnogenesis, see Peel (1989). Examples of nationalist uses of past heroes and sages are described by Kedourie (1971, Introduction); cf. the critiques in Hutchinson (1987, ch. 1), Kapferer (1988) and Roberts (1993), which all focus on the limits to nationalist manipulation set by the social relations moulded by a long history of ethnic and religious ties and sentiments.

15 It is sometimes said that nations require a common destiny, but can manage without a shared history, with the 'new nations' of Asia and Africa being cited as examples. Very often, however, these are new states, not nations, and their ethnic cores can boast a shared history, even if only for a few generations. There are cases, however, where the history in question pertains to a region or province containing several *ethnies* (and religions); but here the sheer power of the shared historical experience of the long struggle for liberation has welded together an ethnically heterogeneous population. Here nationalism functions as a 'religion surrogate' in place of older religions and *ethnies*. An example of this might be Eritrea, though it remains to be seen whether its nationalism can forge a fully fledged nation out of a community of destiny; see Cliffe (1989).

For a similar view of nationalism as concerned with, and seeking 'answers' to, the ultimate issues of mortality and oblivion (and we may add the 'problem of evil'), see Anderson (1983, 17–19).

Bibliography

Ades, Dawn (ed.) (1989): *Art in Latin America: The Modern Era, 1820–1980*, London: South Bank Centre, Hayward Gallery.

Alexander, Stella (1982): 'Religion and national identity in Yugoslavia', in Mews (1982, 591–607).

Allardt, Erik (1979): *Implications of the Ethnic Revival in Modern Industrialised Society: A Comparative Study of Linguistic Minorities in Western Europe, Commentationes Scientiarum Socialium*, Helsinki: Societas Scientiarum Fennica.

Almog, Shmuel (1987): *Zionism and History: The Rise of a New Jewish Consciousness*, Jerusalem: The Magnes Press, Hebrew University, and New York: St Martin's Press.

Almog, Shmuel (1990): *Nationalism and AntiSemitism in Modern Europe, 1815–1945*, Oxford: Pergamon Press.

Alty, J. H. M. (1982): 'Dorians and Ionians', *Journal of Hellenic Studies* 102, 1–14.

Anderson, Benedict (1983): *Imagined Communities: Reflections on the Origins and Spread of Nationalism*, London: Verso Editions and New Left Books.

Anderson, Charles, Mehden, Fred von der and Young, Crawford (1967): *Issues in Political Development*, Englewood Cliffs: Prentice-Hall.

Argyle, W. J. (1976): 'Size and scale as factors in the development of nationalist movements', in A. D. Smith (1976, 31–53).

Armstrong, John (1976): 'Mobilised and proletarian diasporas', *American Political Science Review* 70, 393–408.

Armstrong, John (1982): *Nations before Nationalism*, Chapel Hill: University of North Carolina Press.

Armstrong, John (1992a): 'The autonomy of ethnic identity: historic cleavages and nationality relations in the USSR', in Motyl (1992, 23–43).

Armstrong, John (1992b): 'Nationalism in the former Soviet Empire', *Problems of Communism* XLI, Jan–April, 23–43.

Arnason, Johann (1990): 'Nationalism, globalisation and modernity', in Featherstone (1990, 207–36).

Atiyah, A. S. (1968): *A History of Eastern Christianity*, London: Methuen.

Badcock, Christopher (1991): *Evolution and Individual Behaviour*, Oxford: Blackwell.

Balandier, George (1954): 'Contribution a l'étude des nationalismes en Afrique noire', *Zaire* 8, 379–89.

Banuazizi, Ali and Weiner, Myron (eds) (1986): *The State, Religion and Ethnic Politics: Afganistan, Iran and Pakistan*, Syracuse, New York: Syracuse University Press.

Barth, Fredrik (ed.) (1969): *Ethnic Groups and Boundaries*, Boston: Little, Brown and Company.

Beer, William (1977): 'The social class of ethnic activists in contemporary France', in Esman (1977, 143–58).

Beitz, C. (1979): *Political Theory and International Relations*, Princeton: Princeton University Press.

Bell, Daniel (1975): 'Ethnicity and social change', in Glazer and Moynihan (1975, 141–74).

Bendix, Reinhard (1964): *Nation-Building and Citizenship*, New York: John Wiley.

Bendix, Reinhard (1966): 'Tradition and modernity reconsidered', *Comparative Studies in Society and History* IX, 292–346.

Benthem van den Berghe, G. van (1966): 'Contemporary nationalism in the Western world', *Daedalus* 95, 3, 828–61.

Berger, Suzanne (1977): 'Bretons and Jacobins: reflections on French regional ethnicity', in Esman (1977, 159–78).

Berghe, Pierre van den (1979): *The Ethnic Phenomenon*, New York: Elsevier.

Berlin, Isaiah (1976): *Vico and Herder*, London: Hogarth Press.

Bhabha, Homi (ed.) (1990): *Nation and Narration*, London and New York: Routledge.

Binder, Leonard (1964): *The Ideological Revolution in the Middle East*, New York: John Wiley.

Birch, Anthony (1989): *Nationalism and National Integration*, London: Unwin Hyman.

Blinkhorn, Martin and Veremis, Thanos (eds) (1990): *Modern Greece: Nationalism and Nationality*, Athens: Sage-ELIAMEP.

Bonacich, Edna (1973): 'A theory of middleman minorities', *American Sociological Review* 38, 583–94.

Boyce, George (1982): *Nationalism in Ireland*, London: Croom Helm.

Branch, Michael (ed.) (1985): *Kalevala: The Land of Heroes* (Finnish orig., 1849), trans. W. F. Kirby, London: The Athlone Press, and New Hampshire: Dover.

Brand, Jack (1978): *The Scottish National Movement*, London: Routledge and Kegan Paul.

Brass, Paul (1974): *Language, Religion and Politics in North India*, Cambridge: Cambridge University Press.

Brass, Paul (1979): 'Elite groups, symbol manipulation and ethnic identity among Muslims of South Asia', in Taylor and Yapp (1979, 35–68).

Brass, Paul (1980): 'Ethnic groups and nationalities: the formation, persistence and transformation of ethnic identities', in Sugar (1980, 1–68).

Brass, Paul (ed.) (1985): *Ethnic Groups and the State*, London: Croom Helm.

Braudel, Fernand (1989): *The Identity of France*, vol. I: *History and Environment* (Fr. orig.), trans. Sian Reynold, London: Fontana Press.

Bremmer, Ian and Taras, Ray (eds) (1993): *Nations and Politics in the Soviet Successor States*, Cambridge: Cambridge University Press.

Breuilly, John (1982): *Nationalism and the State*, Manchester: Manchester University Press.

Brock, Peter (1976): *The Slovak National Awakening*, Toronto: Toronto University Press.

Brown, David (1994): *The State and Ethnic Politics in Southeast Asia*, London and New York: Routledge.

Burrage, Michael (1992): 'Mrs Thatcher and the professions: ideology, impact and ironies of an eleven-year confrontation', working papers for Institute of Government Studies, University of California, Berkeley.

Burrows, E. G. (1982): 'Bold forefathers and the cruel step-mother: ideologies of descent in the American Revolution', paper for conference on *Legitimation by Descent*, Paris: Maison des Sciences de l'Homme.

Camps, Miriam (1965): *What Kind of Europe?: The Community since De Gaulle's Veto*, London: Oxford University Press.

Carr, Edward (1945): *Nationalism and After*, London: Oxford University Press.

Castles, Stephen, Cope, Bill, Kalantzis, Mary and Morrissey, Michael (1988): *Mistaken Identity: Multiculturalism and the Demise of Nationalism in Australia*, Sydney, Pluto Press.

Cherniavsky, Michael (1975): 'Russia', in Ranum (1975, 118–43).

Chrypinski, Vincent (1989): 'Church and Nationality in PostWar Poland', in Ramet (1989, 241–63).

Citron, Suzanne (1988): *Le mythe national*, Paris: Presses Ouvriers.

Cliffe, Lionel (1989): 'Forging a nation: the Eritrean experience', *Third World Quarterly* 11, 4, 131–47.

Cobban, Alfred (1945): *Nationalism and National Self-Determination*, London: Oxford University Press.

Cobban, Alfred (1964): *Rousseau and the Modern State*, 2nd edn, London: Allen and Unwin.

Coleman, James (1958): *Nigeria: Background to Nationalism*, Berkeley and Los Angeles: University of California Press.

Colley, Linda (1992): *Britons: Forging the Nation, 1707–1837*, New Haven and London: Yale University Press.

Colls, Robert and Dodd, Philip (eds) (1986): *Englishness: Politics and Culture, 1880–1920*, London: Croom Helm.

Connor, Walker (1972): 'Nation-building or nation-destroying?', *World Politics* XXIV, 319–55.

Connor, Walker (1978): 'A nation is a nation, is a state, is an ethnic group, is a . . .', *Ethnic and Racial Studies* 1, 4, 378–400.

Connor, Walker (1984a): *The National Question in Marxist-Leninist Theory and Strategy*, Princeton: Princeton University Press.

Connor, Walker (1984b): 'Eco- or ethno-nationalism?', *Ethnic and Racial Studies* 7, 3, 342–59.

Connor, Walker (1990): 'When is a nation?', *Ethnic and Racial*

Studies 13, 1, 92–103.

Connor, Walker (1993): 'Beyond reason?: the nature of the ethno-national bond', *Ethnic and Racial Studies* 16, 3, 373–89.

Conversi, Daniele (1990): 'Language or race?: the choice of core values in the development of Catalan and Basque nationalisms', *Ethnic and Racial Studies* 13, 1, 50–70.

Conversi, Daniele (1994): *Language, Immigration and National-ism: Comparing the Catalan and Basque Cases*, unpubd PhD thesis, University of London.

Cook, J. M. (1983): *The Persian Empire*, London: J. M. Dent.

Corrigan, Philip and Sayer, Derek (1985): *The Great Arch: English State Formation as Cultural Revolution*, Oxford: Blackwell.

Crowder, Michael (1968): *West Africa under Colonial Rule*, London: Hutchinson and Co.

Crump, Jeremy (1986): 'The identity of English music: the recep-tion of Elgar (1899–1935)', in Colls and Dodd (1986, 164–90).

Cummins, Ian (1980): *Marx, Engels and National Movements*, London: Croom Helm.

Davies, Norman (1982): *God's Playground: A History of Poland*, 2 vols, Oxford: Clarendon Press.

Davis, Horace (1967): *Nationalism and Socialism: Marxist and Labor Theories of Nationalism*, New York: Monthly Review Press.

Deutsch, Karl (1966): *Nationalism and Social Communication* (1st edn, 1953), 2nd edn, enlarged, Cambridge, Mass., MIT Press.

Deutsch, Karl and Foltz, William (eds) (1963): *Nation-Building*, New York: Atherton.

Dixon, Simon (1990): 'The Russians: the dominant nationality', in G. E. Smith (1990, 21–37).

Doob, Leonard (1964): *Patriotism and Nationalism: Their Psycho-logical Foundations*, New Haven and London: Yale University Press.

Dunlop, John B. (1985): *The New Russian Nationalism*, New York: Praeger.

Duroselle, Jean-Baptiste (1990): *Europe: A History of its Peoples* (Fr. orig.), trans. Richard Mayne, London: Penguin Books.

Edwards, John (1985): *Language, Society and Identity*, Oxford: Basil Blackwell.

Eisenstadt, S. N. (1963): *The Political System of Empires*, New

York: Free Press.

Eisenstadt, S. N. (1965): *Modernisation: Protest and Change*, Englewood Cliffs: Prentice-Hall.

Eller, Jack and Coughlan, Reed (1993): 'The poverty of primordialism: the demystification of ethnic attachments', *Ethnic and Racial Studies* 16, 2, 183–202.

Eri, Gyongyi and Jobbagyi, Zsuzsa (eds) (1989): *A Golden Age: Art and Society in Hungary, 1896–1914*, London: Barbican Art Gallery, Corvina.

Eriksen, Thomas (1993): 'Formal and informal nationalism', *Ethnic and Racial Studies* 16, 1, 1–25.

Esman, Milton (ed.) (1977): *Ethnic Conflict in the Western World*, Ithaca: Cornell University Press.

Fahrni, Dieter (1983): *An Outline History of Switzerland*, Zurich: Pro Helvetia, Arts Council of Switzerland.

Featherstone, Mike (ed.) (1990): *Global Culture: Nationalism, Globalisation and Modernity*, London, Newbury Park and New Delhi: Sage Publications.

Finley, Moses (1986): *The Use and Abuse of History*, London: Hogarth Press.

Fishman, Joshua (1980): 'Social theory and ethnography: neglected perspectives on language and ethnicity in Eastern Europe', in Sugar (1980, 69–99).

Franco, Jean (1970): *The Modern Culture of Latin America*, Harmondsworth: Penguin.

Frye, Richard (1966): *The Heritage of Persia*, New York: Mentor.

Galtung, Johann (1973): *The European Community: A Superpower in the Making*, London: Allen and Unwin.

Gans, Herbert (1979): 'Symbolic ethnicity', *Ethnic and Racial Studies* 2, 1, 1–20.

Geertz, Clifford (1963): 'The integrative revolution', in Clifford Geertz (ed.): *Old Societies and New States*, New York: Free Press.

Geiss, Immanuel (1974): *The PanAfrican Movement*, London: Methuen.

Gella, Alexander (ed.) (1976): *The Intelligentsia and the Intellectuals*, Beverley Hills: Sage Publications.

Gellner, Ernest (1964): *Thought and Change*, London: Weidenfeld and Nicolson.

Gellner, Ernest (1982): 'Nationalism and the two forms of cohesion in complex societies', *Proceedings of the British Academy* 68, London: Oxford University Press.

Gellner, Ernest (1983): *Nations and Nationalism*, Oxford: Basil Blackwell.

Gellner, Ernest (1992): 'Nationalism reconsidered and E. H. Carr', *Review of International Studies* 18, 285–93.

Giddens, Anthony (1985): *The Nation-State and Violence*, Cambridge: Polity Press.

Giddens, Anthony (1991): *The Consequences of Modernity*, Cambridge: Polity Press.

Gildea, Robert (1994): *The Past in French History*, New Haven and London: Yale University Press.

Gladwyn, Lord (1967): *The European Idea*, London: New English Library.

Glazer, Nathan and Moynihan, Daniel (eds) (1975): *Ethnicity: Theory and Experience*, Cambridge, Mass.: Harvard University Press.

Glenny, Mischa (1990): *The Rebirth of History*, Harmondsworth: Penguin.

Gouldner, Alvin (1979): *The Rise of the Intellectuals and the Future of the New Class*, London: Macmillan.

Greenfeld, Liah (1992): *Nationalism: Five Roads to Modernity*, Cambridge, Mass.: Harvard University Press.

Grodzins, Morton (1956): *The Loyal and the Disloyal: The Social Boundaries of Patriotism and Treason*, Cleveland and New York: Meridian Books.

Grosby, Steven (1991): 'Religion and nationality in antiquity', *European Journal of Sociology* XXXII, 229–65.

Grosby, Steven (1994): 'The verdict of history: the inexpungeable tie of primordiality – a response to Eller and Coughlan', *Ethnic and Racial Studies* 17, 1, 164–71.

Guenée, Bernard (1985): *States and Rulers in Later Medieval Europe* (Fr. orig., 1971), trans. Juliet Vale, Oxford: Basil Blackwell.

Gutierrez, Natividad (1995): 'Miscegenation as nation-building: Indian and immigrant women in Mexico', in Nira Yuval-Davis and Daiva Stasiulis (eds): *Unsettling Settler Societies*, London: Sage Publications.

Haas, Ernest (1964): *Beyond the Nation-State: Functionalism and International Organisation*, Stanford: Stanford University Press.

Hall, Raymond (ed.) (1979): *Ethnic Autonomy: Comparative Dynamics*, New York: Pergamon Press.

Halliday, Fred (1979): *Iran: Dictatorship or Development*, Harmondsworth: Penguin.

Hanham, H. J. (1969): *Scottish Nationalism*, London: Faber.

Hechter, Michael (1975): *Internal Colonialism: The Celtic Fringe in British National Development, 1536–1966*, London: Routledge and Kegan Paul.

Hechter, Michael (1987): 'Nationalism as group solidarity', *Ethnic and Racial Studies* 10, 4, 415–26.

Hechter, Michael (1988): 'Rational choice theory and the study of race and ethnic relations', in Rex and Mason (1988, 264–79).

Hechter, Michael (1992): 'The dynamics of secession', *Acta Sociologica* 35, 267–83.

Hechter, Michael and Levi, Margaret (1979): 'The comparative study of ethno-regional movements', *Ethnic and Racial Studies* 2, 3, 260–74.

Held, David et al. (eds) (1985): *States and Societies*, Open University, Oxford: Basil Blackwell.

Heraclides, Alexis (1991): *The Self-Determination of Minorities in International Politics*, London: Frank Cass and Co.

Heraud, Guy (1963): *L'Europe des ethnies*, Paris: Presses d'Europe.

Herbert, Robert (1972): *David, Voltaire, Brutus and the French Revolution*, London: Allen Lane.

Hertzberg, Arthur (ed.) (1960): *The Zionist Idea: A Reader*, New York: Meridian Books.

Hinsley, F. H. (1973): *Nationalism and the International System*, London: Hodder and Stoughton.

Hobsbawm, Eric (1977): 'Some reflections on *The Break-up of Britain*', *New Left Review* 105, 3–23.

Hobsbawm, Eric (1990): *Nations and Nationalism since 1780*, Cambridge: Cambridge University Press.

Hobsbawm, Eric and Ranger, Terence (eds) (1983): *The Invention of Tradition*, Cambridge: Cambridge University Press.

Hoffman, Stanley (1994): 'Europe's identity crisis revisited', *Daedalus (Europe through a Glass Darkly)*, 123, 2, 1–22.

Holmes, R. F. G. (1982): 'Ulster Presbyterians and Irish nationalism', in Mews (1982, 535–48).

Honko, Lauri (1985): 'The *Kalevala* process', *Books from Finland* 19, 1, 16–23.

Horne, Donald (1984): *The Great Museum*, London and Sydney, Pluto Press.

Horowitz, Donald (1985): *Ethnic Groups in Conflict*, Berkeley and Los Angeles, University of California Press.

Hroch, Miroslav (1985): *Social Preconditions of National Revival in Europe*, Cambridge: Cambridge University Press.

Hughes, Michael (1988): *Nationalism and Society: Germany 1800–1945*, London: Edward Arnold.

Husbands, Christopher (1991): 'The support for the *Front National*: analyses and findings', *Ethnic and Racial Studies* 14, 3, 382–416.

Hutchinson, John (1987): *The Dynamics of Cultural Nationalism: The Gaelic Revival and the Creation of the Irish Nation-State*, London: Allen and Unwin.

Ignatieff, Michael (1993): *Blood and Belonging: Journeys into the New Nationalisms*, London, Chatto and Windus.

Igwara, Obi (1993): *State and Nation Building in Nigeria*, unpubd PhD thesis, University of London.

Im Hof, Ulrich (1991): *Mythos Schweiz*, Zurich: Verlag Neue Zürcher Zeitung.

James, Winston (1989): 'The making of black identities', in Samuel (1989, 230–55).

Jelavich, Barbara (1983): *History of the Balkans: Eighteenth and Nineteenth Centuries*, Cambridge: Cambridge University Press.

Jenkins, Richard (1988): 'Social-anthropological models of interethnic relations', in Rex and Mason (1988, 170–86).

Jenkyns, Richard (1992): *Dignity and Decadence: Victorian Art and the Classical Inheritance*, London: Fontana Press.

Johnson, Chalmers (1969): 'Building a communist nation in China', in R. A. Scalapino (ed.) (1969): *The Communist Revolution in Asia*, Englewood Cliffs: Prentice-Hall, 52–84.

Johnson, Harry (ed.) (1968): *Economic Nationalism in Old and New States*, London: Allen and Unwin.

Johnson, Lesley (1992): 'Imagining communities', paper for conference on *Imagining Communities: Medieval and Modern*, Centre for Medieval Studies, University of Leeds.

Just, Roger (1989): 'The triumph of the *Ethnos*', in Tonkin, McDonald and Chapman (1989, 71–88).

Kahan, Arcadius (1968): 'Nineteenth century European experience with policies of economic nationalism', in H. Johnson (1968, 17–30).

Kamenka, Eugene (ed.) (1976): *Nationalism: the Nature and Evolution of an Idea*, London: Edward Arnold.

Kapferer, Bruce (1988): *Legends of People, Myths of State: Violence, Intolerance, and Political Culture in Sri Lanka and Australia*, Washington and London: Smithsonian Institution Press.

Katzenstein, P. (1977): 'Ethnic political conflict in South Tyrol', in Esman (1977, 287–323).

Kautsky, J. H. (ed.) (1962): *Political Change in Underdeveloped Countries*, New York: Wiley.

Keddie, Nikki (1981): *Roots of Revolution: An Interpretive History of Modern Iran*, New Haven and London: Yale University Press.

Kedourie, Elie (1960): *Nationalism*, London: Hutchinson.

Kedourie, Elie (ed.) (1971): *Nationalism in Asia and Africa*, London: Weidenfeld and Nicolson.

Kedourie, Elie (1992): *Politics in the Middle East*, Oxford: Oxford University Press.

Kedward, R. (ed.) (1965): *The Dreyfus Affair*, London: Longman.

Keen, Maurice (1969): *A History of the Middle Ages*, Harmondsworth: Penguin.

Kemilainen, Aira (1964): *Nationalism, Problems concerning the Word, the Concept and Classification*, Yvaskyla: Kustantajat Publishers.

Kirk, G. S. (1973): *Myth, its Meanings and Functions in Ancient and Other Cultures*, Cambridge: Cambridge University Press.

Kitromilides, Paschalis (1989): ' "Imagined communities" and the origins of the national question in the Balkans', *European History Quarterly* 19, 2, 149–92.

Kofos, Evangelos (1990): 'National heritage and national identity in nineteenth and twentieth century Macedonia', in Blinkhorn and Veremis (1990, 103–41).

Kohn, Hans (1940): 'The origins of English nationalism', *Journal of the History of Ideas* I, 69–94.

Kohn, Hans (1957a): *American Nationalism: An Interpretive Essay*, New York: Macmillan.

Kohn, Hans (1957b): *Nationalism and Liberty: The Swiss Example*, New York: Macmillan.

Kohn, Hans (1960): *Pan-Slavism* (1st edn, 1953), 2nd edn, New York: Vintage Books.

Kohn, Hans (1965): *The Mind of Germany*, London: Macmillan.

Kohn, Hans (1967): *The Idea of Nationalism* (1st edn, 1944), 2nd edn, New York: Collier-Macmillan.

Kohr, Leopold (1957): *The Breakdown of Nations*, London: Routledge and Kegan Paul.

Koht, Halvdan (1947): 'The dawn of nationalism in Europe', *American Historical Review* 52, 265–80.

Kreis, Georg (1991): *Der Mythos von 1291: Zur Enstehung des schweizerischen Nationalfeiertags*, Basel: Friedrich Reinhardt Verlag.

Krejci, Yaroslav and Velimsky, Viteslav (1981): *Ethnic and Political Nations in Europe*, London: Croom Helm.

Krol, Marcin (1990): 'A Europe of nations or a universalistic Europe?', *International Affairs* 66, 2, 285–90.

Laczko, Leslie (1994): 'Canada's pluralism in comparative perspective', *Ethnic and Racial Studies* 17, 1, 20–41.

Landau, Jacob (1981): *Pan-Turkism in Turkey*, London: C. Hurst & Co.

Layton, Robert (1985): 'The *Kalevala* and music', *Books from Finland* 19, 1, 56–9.

Lehmann, Jean-Pierre (1982): *The Roots of Modern Japan*, London and Basingstoke: The Macmillan Press Ltd.

Leoussi, Athena (1992): *The Social Significance of Visual Images of Greeks in English and French Art, 1833–80*, unpubd PhD thesis, University of London.

Lerner, Daniel (1958): *The Passing of Traditional Society*, New York: Free Press.

Levi, Mario Attilio (1965): *Political Power in the Ancient World* (It. orig., 1955), trans. J. Costello, London: Weidenfeld and Nicolson.

Lewis, I. M. (ed.) (1983): *Nationalism and Self-Determination in the Horn of Africa*, London: Ithaca Press.

Lewis, W. H. (ed.) (1965): *French-Speaking Africa: The Search for*

Identity, New York: Walker.

Lowenthal, D. (1985): *The Past is a Foreign Country*, Cambridge: Cambridge University Press.

Lyons, F. S. (1979): *Culture and Anarchy in Ireland, 1890–1930*, London: Oxford University Press.

MacIver, D. N. (1982): 'The paradox of nationalism in Scotland', in Williams (1982a, 105–44).

Mack Smith, Denis (1994): *Mazzini*, New Haven and London: Yale University Press.

Macmillan, Duncan (1986): *Painting in Scotland: The Golden Age*, Oxford: Phaidon Press.

McNeill, William (1986): *Polyethnicity and National Unity in World History*, Toronto: University of Toronto Press.

Mallory, J. P. (1989): *In Search of the Indo-Europeans: Language, Archaeology and Myth*, London: Thames and Hudson.

Mandel, Ernest (1975): 'The nation-state and imperialism', in Held et al. (1985, 526–39).

Mann, Michael (1986): *The Sources of Social Power*, vol. I, Cambridge: Cambridge University Press.

Markovitz, I. L. (1977): *Power and Class in Africa*, Englewood Cliffs: Prentice-Hall.

Martin, David (1978): *A General Theory of Secularisation*, Oxford: Basil Blackwell.

Marwick, Arthur (1974): *War and Social Change in the Twentieth Century*, London: Methuen.

Mayall, James (1990): *Nationalism and International Society*, Cambridge: Cambridge University Press.

Mayo, Patricia (1974): *The Roots of Identity: Three National Movements in Contemporary European Politics*, London: Allen Lane.

Mazrui, Ali (1966): *Towards a Pax Africana*, London: Weidenfeld and Nicolson.

Meadwell, Hudson (1989): 'Cultural and instrumental approaches to ethnic nationalism', *Ethnic and Racial Studies* 12, 3, 309–28.

Medhurst, Ken (1982): 'Basques and Basque nationalism', in Williams (1982a, 235–61).

Melucci, Alberto (1989): *Nomads of the Present: Social Movements and Individual Needs in Contemporary Society*, London: Hutchinson Radius.

Mendels, Doron (1992): *The Rise and Fall of Jewish Nationalism*, New York: Doubleday.

Merritt, Richard and Rokkan, Stein (1966): *Comparing Nations: The Use of Quantitative Data in Cross-National Research*, New Haven: Yale University Press.

Mews, Stuart (ed.) (1982): *Religion and National Identity*, Studies in Church History, vol. 18, Oxford: Basil Blackwell.

Miles, Robert (ed.) (1993): 'Migration and the New Europe', in *Ethnic and Racial Studies* 16, 3, 459–562.

Miles, Robert and Singer-Kerel, Jeanne (eds) (1991): *Migration and Migrants in France*, special issue, *Ethnic and Racial Studies* 14, 3.

Miller, David (1993): 'In defence of nationality', *Journal of Applied Philosophy* 10, 1, 3–16.

Minogue, Kenneth (1967a): *Nationalism*, London: Batsford.

Minogue, Kenneth (1967b): 'Nationalism: the poverty of a concept', *European Journal of Sociology* VIII, 332–43.

Mitchell, Marion (1931): 'Emile Durkheim and the philosophy of nationalism', *Political Science Quarterly* 46, 87–106.

Mitchison, Rosalind (ed.) (1980): *The Roots of Nationalism: Studies in Northern Europe*, Edinburgh: John Donald Publishers.

Moore, R. I. (1987): *The Formation of a Persecuting Society: Power and Deviance in Western Europe, 950–1250*, Oxford: Basil Blackwell.

Morgan, Kenneth (1982): *Rebirth of a Nation: Wales 1880–1980*, Oxford: Oxford University Press.

Morgan, Prys (1983): 'From a death to a view: the hunt for the Welsh past in the Romantic period', in Hobsbawm and Ranger (1983, 43–100).

Moscati, Sabatino (1962): *The Face of the Ancient Orient*, New York: Anchor Books.

Moscati, Sabatino (1973): *The World of the Phoenicians*, London: Cardinal, Sphere Books Ltd.

Mosse, George (1964): *The Crisis of German Ideology*, New York: Grosset and Dunlap.

Mosse, George (1976): 'Mass politics and the political liturgy of nationalism', in Kamenka (1976, 39–54).

Motyl, Alexander (1992): *Thinking Theoretically about Soviet Nationalities: History and Comparison in the Study of the USSR*, New York: Columbia University Press.

Mouzelis, Nicos (1990): *Post-Marxist Alternatives*, London: Macmillan Press.

Nairn, Tom (1977): *The Breakup of Britain: Crisis and Neo-Nationalism*, London: New Left Books.

Nash, Manning (1989): *The Cauldron of Ethnicity in the Modern World*, Chicago and London: University of Chicago Press.

Nettl, J. P. and Robertson, R. (1968): *International Systems and the Modernisation of Societies*, London: Faber.

Neuberger, Benjamin (1986): *National Self-Determination in Post-Colonial Africa*, Boulder, Colorado: Lynne Rienner Publishers.

Neusner, Jacob (1981): *Max Weber Revisited: Religion and Society in Ancient Judaism*, Oxford: Oxford Centre for Postgraduate Hebrew Studies.

Newman, Gerald (1987): *The Rise of English Nationalism: A Cultural History, 1740–1830*, London: Weidenfeld and Nicolson.

O'Brien, Conor Cruise (1988): *God-Land: Reflections on Religion and Nationalism*, Cambridge, Mass.: Harvard University Press.

Okamura, J. Y. (1981): 'Situational ethnicity', *Ethnic and Racial Studies* 4, 4, 452–65.

Orridge, Andrew (1980): 'Varieties of nationalisms', in Tivey (1980, 39–58).

Orridge, Andrew (1981): 'Uneven development and nationalism, I and II', *Political Studies* XXIX, 1 and 2, 1–15, 181–90.

Orridge, Andrew (1982): 'Separatist and autonomist nationalisms: the structure of regional loyalties in the modern state', in Williams (1982a, 43–74).

Orridge, Andrew and Williams, Colin (1982): 'Autonomist nationalism: a theoretical framework for spatial variations in its genesis and development', *Political Geography Quarterly* 1, 1, 19–39.

Paul, David (1985): 'Slovak nationalism and the Hungarian state', in Brass (1985, 115–59).

Payne, Stanley (1971): 'Catalan and Basque nationalism', *Journal of Contemporary History* 6, 15–51.

Pearson, Raymond (1993): 'Fact, fantasy, fraud: perceptions and projections of national revival', *Ethnic Studies* 10, 1–3, 43–64 (special issue on *Pre-Modern and Modern National Identity in Russia and Eastern Europe*, edited by Wendy Bracewell, Tamara Dragadze and Anthony Smith).

Peel, John (1989): 'The cultural work of Yoruba ethnogenesis', in Tonkin, McDonald and Chapman (1989, 198–215).

Petrovich, Michael (1980): 'Religion and ethnicity in Eastern Europe', in Sugar (1980, 373–417).

Pinard, Maurice and Hamilton, Richard (1982): 'The Quebec Independence movement', in Williams (1982a, 203–33).

Pinard, Maurice and Hamilton, Richard (1984): 'The class bases of the Quebec Independence movement: conjectures and evidence', *Ethnic and Racial Studies* 7, 1, 19–54.

Plamenatz, John (1976): 'Two types of nationalism', in Kamenka (1976, 22–36).

Poliakov, Leon (1974): *The Aryan Myth*, New York: Basic Books.

Porter, John (1965): *The Vertical Mosaic*, Toronto: University of Toronto Press.

Porter, Roy and Teich, Mikulas (eds) (1988): *Romanticism in National Context*, Cambridge: Cambridge University Press.

Posen, Barry (1993): 'The security dilemma and ethnic conflict', *Survival* 35, 1, 27–47.

Pospielovsky, Dimitry (1989): 'The "Russian orientation" and the Orthodox Church: from the early Slavophiles to the '"Neo-Slavophiles" in the USSR', in Ramet (1989, 81–108).

Pynsent, Robert (1994): *Questions of Identity: Czech and Slovak Ideas of Nationality and Personality*, London: Central European University Press.

Ramet, Pedro (ed.) (1989): *Religion and Nationalism in Soviet and East European Politics*, Durham, NC, and London: Duke University Press.

Ranum, Orest (ed.) (1975): *National Consciousness, History and Political Culture in Early Modern Europe*, Baltimore and London: Johns Hopkins University Press.

Raynor, Henry (1976): *Music and Society since 1815*, London: Barrie and Jenkins.

Reiss, H. S. (ed.) (1955): *The Political Thought of the German Romantics, 1793–1815*, Oxford: Blackwell.

Renan, Ernest (1882): *Qu'est-ce qu'une nation?*, Paris: Calmann-Levy.

Renfrew, Colin (1987): *Archaeology and Language: The Puzzle of Indo-European Origins*, London: Jonathan Cape.

Rex, John and Mason, David (eds) (1988): *Theories of Race and*

Ethnic Relations (1st edn, 1986), paperback reprint, Cambridge: Cambridge University Press.

Reynolds, Susan (1984): *Kingdoms and Communities in Western Europe, 900–1300*, Oxford: Clarendon.

Reynolds, V. (1980): 'Sociobiology and the idea of primordial discrimination', *Ethnic and Racial Studies* 3, 3, 303–15.

Richmond, Anthony (1984): 'Ethnic nationalism and postindustrialism', *Ethnic and Racial Studies* 7, 1, 4–18.

Rickard, P. (1974): *A History of the French Language*, London: Hutchinson University Library.

Roberts, Michael (1993): 'Nationalism, the past and the present: the case of Sri Lanka', *Ethnic and Racial Studies* 16, 1, 133–66.

Robson-Scott, W. D. (1965): *The Literary Background of the Gothic Revival in Germany*, Oxford: Clarendon.

Rosdolsky, R. (1964): 'Friedrich Engels und das Problem der "Geschichtslosen Völker"', *Archiv für Sozialgeschichte* 4, 87–282 (Hanover).

Rosenblum, Robert (1967): *Transformations in Late Eighteenth Century Art*, Princeton: Princeton University Press.

Rosenthal, Erwin (1965): *Islam and the Modern National State*, Cambridge: Cambridge University Press.

Rougemont, Denis de (1965): *The Meaning of Europe*, London: Sidgwick and Jackson.

Royal Academy of Arts (1979): *Post-Impressionism*, London: Weidenfeld and Nicolson, for the Royal Academy.

Samuel, Raphael (ed.) (1989): *Patriotism, the Making and Unmaking of British National Identity*, London and New York: Routledge.

Saunders, David (1993): 'What makes a nation a nation?: Ukrainians since 1600', *Ethnic Studies* 10, 1, 101–24 (special issue).

Schama, Simon (1987): *The Embarrassment of Riches: An Interpretation of Dutch Culture in the Golden Age*, London: William Collins.

Schermerhorn, Richard (1970): *Comparative Ethnic Relations*, New York: Random House.

Schlesinger, Philip (1987): 'On national identity: some conceptions and misconceptions criticised', *Social Science Information Bulletin* 26, 2, 219–64.

Schlesinger, Philip (1992): 'Europe – a new cultural battlefield?', *Innovation* 5, 1, 11–23.

Schlesinger, Philip (1994): 'Europe's contradictory communicative space', *Daedalus (Europe through a Glass Darkly)*, 123, 2, 25–52.

Segre, Dan (1980): *A Crisis of Identity: Israel and Zionism*, London: Oxford University Press.

Seton-Watson, Hugh (1977): *Nations and States: An Inquiry into the Origins of Nations and the Politics of Nationalism*, London: Methuen.

Sharabi, Hisham (1970): *The Arab Intellectuals and the West: The Formative Years, 1875–1914*, Baltimore and London: Johns Hopkins University Press.

Shils, Edward (1957): 'Primordial, personal, sacred and civil ties', *British Journal of Sociology* 7, 113–45.

Shils, Edward (1960): 'The intellectuals in the political development of the new states', *World Politics* 12, 329–68.

Singleton, F. (1985): *A Short History of the Yugoslav Peoples*, Cambridge: Cambridge University Press.

Sklair, Leslie (1991): *Sociology of the Global System*, Baltimore: Johns Hopkins University Press.

Smelser, Neil (1968): *Essays in Sociological Explanation*, Englewood Cliffs: Prentice-Hall.

Smith, Anthony D. (1971): *Theories of Nationalism*, London, Duckworth, and New York: Harper and Row.

Smith, Anthony D. (1973): 'Nationalism: a trend report and annotated bibliography', *Current Sociology* 21, 3, 1–178, The Hague: Mouton.

Smith, Anthony D. (ed.) (1976): *Nationalist Movements*, London: Macmillan Press Ltd.

Smith, Anthony D. (1979a): *Nationalism in the Twentieth Century*, Oxford: Martin Robertson.

Smith, Anthony D. (1979b): 'The "historical revival" in late eighteenth century England and France', *Art History* 2, 2, 156–78.

Smith, Anthony D. (1981a): *The Ethnic Revival in the Modern World*, Cambridge: Cambridge University Press.

Smith, Anthony D. (1981b): 'War and ethnicity: the role of warfare in the formation, self-images and cohesion of ethnic communities', *Ethnic and Racial Studies* 4, 4, 375–97.

Smith, Anthony D. (1982): 'Nationalism, ethnic separatism and the intelligentsia', in Williams (1982a, 17–41).

Smith, Anthony D. (1983): 'Nationalism and classical social theory', *British Journal of Sociology* 34, 1, 19–38.

Smith, Anthony D. (1984): 'National identity and myths of ethnic descent', *Research in Social Movements, Conflict and Change* 7, 95–130.

Smith, Anthony D. (1985): '*Ethnie* and nation in the modern world', *Millennium: Journal of International Studies* 14, 2, 127–42.

Smith, Anthony D. (1986a): *The Ethnic Origins of Nations*, Oxford: Basil Blackwell.

Smith, Anthony D. (1986b): 'History and liberty: dilemmas of loyalty in Western democracies', *Ethnic and Racial Studies* 9, 1, 43–65.

Smith, Anthony D. (1987): *Patriotism and Neo-Classicism: The 'Historical Revival' in French and English Painting and Sculpture, 1746–1800*, unpubd PhD thesis, University of London.

Smith, Anthony D. (1988): 'The myth of the "modern nation" and the myths of nations', *Ethnic and Racial Studies* 11, 1, 1–26.

Smith, Anthony D. (1989): 'The origins of nations', *Ethnic and Racial Studies* 12, 3, 340–67.

Smith, Anthony D. (1990a): 'The supersession of nationalism?', *International Journal of Comparative Sociology* XXXI, 1–2, 1–31.

Smith, Anthony D. (1990b): 'Towards a Global Culture?', in Featherstone (1990, 171–91).

Smith, Anthony D. (1991): *National Identity*, London: Penguin.

Smith, Anthony D. (1992a): 'Chosen peoples: why ethnic groups survive', *Ethnic and Racial Studies* 15, 3, 436–56.

Smith, Anthony D. (1992b): 'Nationalism and the historians', *International Journal of Comparative Sociology* XXXIII, 1–2, 58–80.

Smith, Anthony D. (1992c): 'The question of Jewish identity', *Studies in Contemporary Jewry* 8, 219–33.

Smith, Anthony D. (1992d): 'National identity and the idea of European unity', *International Affairs* 68, 1, 55–76.

Smith, Anthony D. (1993a): 'Art and nationalism in Europe', in *De onmacht van het grote: Cultuur in Europa*, ed. J. C. H. Blom et al., Amsterdam: Amsterdam University Press, 64–80.

Smith, Anthony D. (1993b): 'Ethnic election and cultural identity', *Ethnic Studies* 10, 1–3, 9–25 (special issue).

Smith, Anthony D. (1994): 'The problem of national identity: ancient, medieval and modern?', *Ethnic and Racial Studies* 17, 3, 375–99.

Smith, Anthony D. and Williams, Colin (1983): 'The national construction of social space', *Progress in Human Geography* 7, 4, 502–18.

Smith, Donald E. (ed.) (1974): *Religion and Political Modernisation*, New Haven: Yale University Press.

Smith, Graham E. (1989): 'Gorbachev's greatest challenge: *perestroika* and the national question', *Political Geography Quarterly* 8, 1, 7–20.

Smith, Graham E. (ed.) (1990): *The Nationalities Question in the Soviet Union*, London and New York: Longman.

Snyder, Louis (1954): *The Meaning of Nationalism*, New Brunswick: Rutgers University Press.

Snyder, Jack (1993): 'Nationalism and the crisis of the post-Soviet state', *Survival* 35, 1, 5–26.

Stack, J. F. (ed.) (1986): *The Primordial Challenge: Ethnicity in the Contemporary World*, New York: Greenwood Press.

Stavrianos, L. S. (1961): *The Balkans since 1453*, New York: Holt.

Steinberg, Jonathan (1976): *Why Switzerland?*, Cambridge: Cambridge University Press.

Stone, John (ed.) (1979): *Internal Colonialism*, special issue, *Ethnic and Racial Studies* 2, 3.

Sugar, Peter (ed.) (1980): *Ethnic Diversity and Conflict in Eastern Europe*, Santa Barbara: ABC-Clio.

Sugar, Peter and Lederer, Ivo (eds) (1969): *Nationalism in Eastern Europe*, Far Eastern and Russian Institute, Publications on Russia and Eastern Europe, no. 1, Seattle and London: University of Washington Press.

Taylor, David and Yapp, Malcolm (eds) (1979): *Political Identity in South Asia*, London and Dublin: SOAS, Curzon Press Ltd.

Thaden, E. C. (1964): *Conservative Nationalism in Nineteenth Century Russia*, Seattle: University of Washington Press.

Thompson, Leonard (1985): *The Political Mythology of Apartheid*,

New Haven and London: Yale University Press.

Thurer, Georg (1970): *Free and Swiss*, London: Oswald Wolff.

Tilly, Charles (ed.) (1975): *The Formation of National States in Western Europe*, Princeton: Princeton University Press.

Tipton, Leon (ed.) (1972): *Nationalism in the Middle Ages*, New York: Holt, Rinehart and Winston.

Tiryakian, Edward and Rogowski, Ronald (eds) (1985): *New Nationalisms of the Developed West*, London: Allen and Unwin.

Tivey, Leonard (ed.) (1980): *The Nation-State*, Oxford: Martin Robertson.

Tomlinson, John (1991): *Cultural Imperialism*, London: Pinter Publishers.

Tonkin, Elisabeth, McDonald, Maryon and Chapman, Malcolm (eds) (1989): *History and Ethnicity*, ASA Monographs 27, London: Routledge.

Tudor, Henry (1972): *Political Myth*, London: Pall Mall Press Ltd/ Macmillan.

Tuveson, E. L. (1968): *Redeemer Nation: The Idea of America's Millennial Role*, Chicago and London: University of Chicago Press.

Vardys, Stanley (1989): 'Lithuanian national politics', *Problems of Communism* XXXVIII, July–August, 53–76.

Vatikiotis, P. J. (1969): *A Modern History of Egypt*, New York and Washington: Frederick A. Praeger.

Vital, David (1975): *The Origins of Zionism*, Oxford: Clarendon Press.

Vos, George de and Romanucci-Rossi, Lola (eds) (1975): *Ethnic Identity: Cultural Continuities and Change*, Chicago: University of Chicago Press.

Waever, Ole (1992): 'Nordic nostalgia: Northern Europe after the Cold War', *International Affairs* 68, 1, 77–102.

Walker, Christopher (1980): *Armenia, the Survival of a Nation*, London: Routledge.

Wallace, William (1990): *The Transformation of Western Europe*, London: RIIA/Pinter.

Warburton, T. Rennie (1976): 'Nationalism and language in Switzerland and Canada', in A. D. Smith (1976).

Ware, Timothy (1984): *The Orthodox Church*, Harmondsworth: Penguin.

Warren, Bill (1980): *Imperialism, Pioneer of Capitalism*, New York: Monthly Review Press.

Webb, Keith (1977): *The Growth of Nationalism in Scotland*, Harmondsworth: Penguin.

Weber, Eugen (1966): 'The men of the archangel', *Journal of Contemporary History* I, 1, 101–26.

Weber, Eugen (1979): *Peasants into Frenchmen: The Modernisation of Rural France, 1870–1914*, London: Chatto and Windus.

Weber, Eugen (1991): *My France: Politics, Culture, Myth*, Cambridge, Mass.: Harvard University Press.

Weber, Max (1947): *From Max Weber: Essays in Sociology*, ed. Hans Gerth and C. Wright Mills, London: Routledge and Kegan Paul.

Webster, Leslie and Backhouse, Janet (eds) (1991): *The Making of England: Anglo-Saxon Art and Culture*, AD 600–900, London: British Museum Press.

Wiberg, Hakan (1983): 'Self-determination as an international issue', in I. M. Lewis (1983, 43–65).

Wilkinson, Paul (1983): *The New Fascists*, London and Sydney: Pan Books.

Williams, Colin (1977): 'Non-violence and the development of the Welsh Language Society, 1962–74', *Welsh Historical Review* 8, 26–55.

Williams, Colin (ed.) (1982a): *National Separatism*, Cardiff: University of Wales Press.

Williams, Colin (1982b): 'Separatism and the mobilisation of Welsh national identity', in Williams (1982a, 145–201).

Yoshino, Kosaku (1992): *Cultural Nationalism in Contemporary Japan*, London and New York: Routledge.

Young, Crawford (1985): 'Ethnicity and the colonial and post-colonial state in Africa', in Brass (1985, 57–93).

Yuval-Davis, Nira (1993): 'Gender and nation', *Ethnic and Racial Studies* 16, 4, 621–32.

Zartmann, William (1963): *Government and Politics in Northern Africa*, New York: Praeger.

Zenner, Walter (1991): *Minorities in the Middle: A Cross-Cultural Analysis*, Albany: State University of New York Press.

Zolberg, Aristide (1977): 'Splitting the difference: federalisation without federalism in Belgium', in Esman (1977, 103–42).

Index

Entries in italic type indicate where the subject in
question is discussed in detail.